T0331212

In this compelling collaboration, authors Tan and Grandjean present a groundbreaking exploration of the fundamental pillars of economic growth. Through meticulous research and insightful analysis, they illuminate the critical role of human values in shaping thriving economies. A must-read for policymakers, business leaders, and anyone seeking to understand the enduring principles that underpin sustainable economic growth.

Abdulla bin Adel Fakhro
Minister Of Industry and Commerce Bahrain
Kingdom of Bahrain

By the authors' own admission, this book makes bold assertions which may be at odds with most predictions. Using a measuring template based on four key values — work, thrift, trust and risk-talking — they analyse twelve countries, their past successes and failures, prescribe improving ideas for each, and assess their future prospects. The reader may dispute specific arguments in the chapters but is constantly challenged to re-think his own assumptions and preconceptions. If nothing else, the book provides masterly summaries of the economic condition of a comprehensive sampling of countries from a wide spectrum. But it is much more than that; it offers a view of the current state of the world filled with thought-provoking insights.

George Yeo
Former Foreign Minister of Singapore

The authors use twelve well-chosen national case studies to focus a bright light on the interplay of structural and human factors that can generate or inhibit economic growth and broad-based prosperity. By bringing frank and at times provocative observations about cultural values into the traditional economist's analysis of geography, technology, and national policies, this work raises fresh, important questions for analysts and policymakers about the ingredients for national success. Encouragingly in these pessimistic times, the authors succeed in avoiding an overly deterministic approach, acknowledging the potential of human agency to change outcomes, and their sincere concern for humanity at all levels of global society comes through in vivid prose. This is a thought-provoking contribution to the global study of economic and societal success.

Jeff Nankivell
President & CEO
Asia Pacific Foundation of Canada

Having worked with ChinHwee as a fellow board member in India over many years, I have first hand experience of his insightful observations and in depth experience. His decades of operational and financial insights make this unique book a must read for any student of behavioral finance and how it works in the real world.

Naina Lal Kidwai
Former President of the Federation of Indian
Chambers of Commerce and Industry
Republic of India

In a world where economic landscapes are as diverse as the cultures that shape them, understanding the intricate interplay of values and policies becomes paramount. This anthology, meticulously crafted by Tan ChinHwee and Thomas Grandjean, offers a profound exploration into the economic trajectories of 12 countries, delving deep into their stories from the perspective of their 'Values at the Core — Hard Work, Thrift, Trust and Risk Taking' that underpin their successes and shortcomings, showing values as no mere abstract concept; but the unseen hands that shape economic behavior. South Korea is one of these testaments to the virtue of thrift, which has fostered a culture of fiscal discipline that shields the nation from the pitfalls of reckless spending. Hard work has been the unique trait of South Koreans, which enabled the country to become a current economic powerhouse from the ashes of the Korean war. Trust in the Korean society has evolved with the development of modern institutions and social systems, resulting in a more transparent country. Risk-taking, with the government's incentives, has been the driving force transforming South Korea from a predominantly agricultural country in the 1950s into a sophisticated industrial one today. As we navigate an increasingly interconnected world fraught with challenges and opportunities, may this book provide a fresh perspective to their readers on how the economies are being shaped around them and serve as a useful reference for future leaders and policymakers alike.

Ryu Peob Min
Director General for FTA Negotiations
Ministry of Trade, Industry and Energy Republic of Korea

This carefully researched book views the history and prospects of twelve extremely different economies through four societal prisms: their work, thrift, trust, and risk-taking characteristics. You probably will not agree with all of their conclusions, but they certainly warrant careful consideration. Despite its vast scope, this is a relatively easy read.

Wilbur Ross
US Secretary of Commerce
2017–2021 and Author of Risks & Rewards

This new book by ChinHwee Tan and Thomas Grandjean promises a thought-provoking journey chronicling the rise of 12 nations. It offers a fresh perspective that national policies, technological development, culture, geography and human values are not just parallel forces but deeply intertwined in shaping a country's destiny. In engaging case studies, the authors invite readers to consider the delicate balance between national policies that incentivize hard work and the inherent values of societies such as hard work, thrift and risk-taking. This book is a must-read for anyone interested in the multifaceted nature of economic development, and highly relevant for scholars and general interest readers alike.

Juliana Chan
Young Global Leader, World Economic Forum; Founder and CEO
Wildtype Media Group

ChinHwee Tan and Thomas Grandjean take us on a journey from Brazil to Botswana, Sweden to Singapore — a total of twelve nations in all — demonstrating how some simple core values have delivered impactful economic and social outcomes. They provide compelling and wide-ranging examples, across different geographies and cultures, alluding that an education of core values initially ingrained by parents and religious teachers onto young children, later reinforced and burnished in schools and universities, can all sum up to policies that shape the economic trajectories and destinies of our countries. If classical economic theory has a soft side, then this book provides a framework that defines it, in a story-telling and engaging fashion.

Kenneth G. Pereira
Managing Director, Hibiscus Petroleum Berhad

By focusing on the human dynamics behind pure economic data, Grandjean and Tan offer a remarkable insight into how different countries develop and prosper. An increasingly fractured world requires leaders who see beyond their national borders. At such times, getting the right policies in place becomes ever more critical. Invigorating and articulate, blending historical perspective with geopolitical prognostication, this book provides unique messages for both business and government leaders.

Amelia Xiao Fu
Chief Economist, Bank of China International

Work ethic, Trust and Enterprise. Having seeing first hand how Tan worked as a successful fund manager, he and Grandjean succinctly argue that these values can explain what makes or breaks a country. Surveying 12 countries through that lens, the authors offer thought provoking insights that challenge the norms. A useful framework for investors to develop a differentiated way to understanding economies and countries.

Lim Jit Soon CFA
Managing Director
Singapore sovereign wealth fund

Tan and Grandjean have written a book both fascinating and useful. They masterfully take the reader through the factors that have lead to the successful development of various nations. Their key finding — that values has played a large role in progress — is one for policymakers and citizens to internalize.

Paul Bernard CFA
Retired partner
Former head of research for Goldman Sachs

ECONOMIC SUCCESS
Fate or Destiny?

**VALUES AND POLICIES ACROSS 12
COUNTRIES TO BETTER UNDERSTAND THE
WORLD WE LIVE IN**

ECONOMIC SUCCESS
Fate or Destiny?

VALUES AND POLICIES ACROSS 12
COUNTRIES TO BETTER UNDERSTAND THE
WORLD WE LIVE IN

Thomas Grandjean | ChinHwee Tan

Foreword by
General The Lord Richards of Herstmonceux

World Scientific

NEW JERSEY · LONDON · SINGAPORE · BEIJING · SHANGHAI · HONG KONG · TAIPEI · CHENNAI · TOKYO

Published by

World Scientific Publishing Co. Pte. Ltd.

5 Toh Tuck Link, Singapore 596224

USA office: 27 Warren Street, Suite 401-402, Hackensack, NJ 07601

UK office: 57 Shelton Street, Covent Garden, London WC2H 9HE

Library of Congress Control Number: 2024020932

British Library Cataloguing-in-Publication Data
A catalogue record for this book is available from the British Library.

ECONOMIC SUCCESS: FATE OR DESTINY?
Values and Policies Across 12 Countries to Better Understand the World We Live in

ISBN 978-981-12-9494-5 (hardcover)
ISBN 978-981-12-9495-2 (ebook for institutions)
ISBN 978-981-12-9496-9 (ebook for individuals)

For any available supplementary material, please visit
https://www.worldscientific.com/worldscibooks/10.1142/13893#t=suppl

Desk Editors: Sanjay Varadharajan/Kura Sunaina

Typeset by Stallion Press
Email: enquiries@stallionpress.com

Printed in Singapore

Foreword by General
The Lord Richards of
Herstmonceux GCB CBE DSO

In the tumultuous landscape of history, nations rise and fall, their destinies shaped by the collective values and aspirations of their people. As a British Army officer serving in various parts of the world, I have come to appreciate the profound impact that values have on the success and resilience of nations.

In the pages that follow, you will embark on a journey through time and across continents, delving into the stories of nations whose destinies were transformed by their adherence to timeless principles. From the bustling streets of metropolises to the serene landscapes of rural heartlands, these narratives illuminate the diverse tapestry of human endeavor.

At the heart of these stories lies the essence of what it means to be human: the relentless pursuit of progress, the courage to venture into the unknown, the trust that binds communities together, and the wisdom to steward resources with prudence. Each tale serves as a testament to the enduring power of values to shape the course of history.

From the industrious spirit of a nation built on the foundations of hard work to the audacious dreams of pioneers who dared to defy convention, these narratives offer valuable insights into the factors that underpin success on a national scale. They remind us that while the challenges we face may be daunting, they are not insurmountable — so long as we remain steadfast in our commitment to the principles that have guided the best of humanity through the ages.

As you immerse yourself in these stories, I invite you to reflect on the values that define your own journey. For it is through understanding the triumphs and tribulations of others that we gain clarity about our own path forward. May this book inspire you to embrace the values that have the power to shape nations and transform lives.

About the Authors

ChinHwee Tan is Chairman of the Advisory Panel of Singapore's Energy Market Authority and SG Tradex Services. Prior to that, he was Asia-Pacific CEO of a global Fortune 15 company for 8 years and was also Founding Asia Partner of one of the top three largest alternative investors in the world. He is a part of the special taskforce appointed by the Prime Minister's Office to reconfigure Singapore's economy and he sits on various private and public boards and committees, including the Monetary Authority of Singapore. ChinHwee co-wrote the best-selling *Asian Financial Statement Analysis: Detecting Financial Irregularities* and *Values at the Core: How Human Values Contribute to the Rise of Nations*, which was nominated to the Financial Times Readers' Best 2021 Summer Books list. He accepts pro bono cases from regulators across the globe. He is a chartered financial analyst and chartered accountant, and fought the battle to have the words "for the benefit of society" included in the charter as President of CFA Singapore. Together with his wife, he has engaged in social work for years, and he enjoys spending time with his three children.

Thomas Grandjean has worked in the commodities sector for the past 20 years. He graduated with a Master of Science degree in Economics from the University of Lausanne, Switzerland, and is a CFA charterholder. He has lived in the Middle East, the United Kingdom, and Switzerland, and currently resides in Singapore. He co-authored the book *Values at the Core: How Human Values Contribute to the Rise of Nations*.

Praise for *Values at the Core: How Human Values Contribute to the Rise of Nations*:

A thought-provoking book, bringing readers outside their comfort zones.
— *Financial Times Readers' Best 2021 Summer Books*

A highly readable book that provides important messages both for business and government leaders.
— Esko Aho, *Former Prime Minister of Finland*

Using vivid examples from around the world, Grandjean and Tan show that values play a crucial role in shaping the economic success of a country — a compelling antidote to the usual litany of purely economic factors.
— Lord Mervyn King, *Former Governor of the Bank of England*

A practical analysis of the vital indicators which measure the health and vitality of a society.
— George Yeo, *Former Foreign Minister of Singapore*

A brave attempt to combine cultural values with economics. Definitely worth a read.
— Mark Machin, *President, Canada Pension Plan Investment Board*

Elucidates how values come to shape economies and humanity.
— Subra Suresh, *President, Nanyang Technological University, Singapore*

A compelling case that human values are a critical determinant of economic prosperity.
— Jean-Baptiste Michau, *Professor of Economics, Ecole Polytechnique, Paris, France*

A radically different perspective.
— Amelia Xiao Fu, *Chief Economist, Bank of China International*

Warrants wide readership.
— Sir Paul Tucker, *Professor, Harvard Kennedy School* and author of *Unelected Power*

Contents

Differences in habits and attitudes are differences in human capital, just as much as differences in knowledge and skills — and such differences create differences in economic outcomes.[1]

If you put in an enormous amount of work, you're going to have a tremendous advantage over people who don't.[2]

Thomas Sowell

Introduction

China will become a highly developed nation within the next 30 years, with or without a democracy. India is likely to get there as well, but it will take much longer unless the country removes some of its more crippling regulations. North Korea will become a highly industrialized nation within two or three generations if it ever introduces much-needed market reforms. Japan's economy will never escape its ongoing lethargy and will experience several more lost decades. With the possible exception of financial and trading centers such as Dubai, Middle Eastern economies will collapse if oil and gas revenues were to fall significantly. Despite growing concerns from part of its population, the US is not in decline, but it struggles to come to terms with the fact that other large nations are quickly catching up. American consumers will continue to be financed by Asian savers. Southern Europe will never fully catch up to Northern Europe, despite a common market. With very few exceptions, no country in Latin America or in Africa will ever join the ranks of highly industrialized nations.

Those are bold assertions, at odds with most predictions. A common expectation, mostly prevalent in western circles, is that China will fall into the "middle-income trap" unless it adopts democratic institutions. Japan's current predicament is seen as an anomaly that should be resolved by adequate fiscal and monetary policies and further market reforms.

The world's poorest countries are expected to catch up and eventually become highly developed themselves, if only they adopted democratic institutions, introduced market reforms, embraced globalization, and rid themselves of their dependency to natural resources. We strongly disagree with those predictions.

Theories on international development typically focus on one of three factors: policies, geography, and culture. Most authors dismiss geography and culture and only focus on policies: strong democratic institutions, market forces, education, fighting corruption, and sound fiscal and monetary policies.

Geography did play an important role in the past: Societies then were much more likely to expand and accumulate wealth when surrounded by flat and fertile land, having access to the sea or a river, being germ-free, and benefiting from a temperate climate. But the role of geography has become much more limited with technological progress. Growth can now take place in most environments except for the most extreme ones (developing a large, prosperous society in Antarctica or at high altitudes remains improbable). One example of technology enabling improved standards of living in more challenging environments is the air-conditioning unit, a device invented in the early twentieth century. Southern states in the US, the Middle East, or Singapore would not have prospered as much as they did without air-conditioning.

Then, there is "culture," a loose concept that has always been difficult to define. We instead refer to *values*, defined as principles that we closely identify with, acquired during our youth and which drive us throughout our lives. Human values are too often neglected: They are complex, messy, and hard to measure. They do not lend themselves well to beautiful mathematical equations. But if we leave values out of the equation, we are missing out on a vital aspect of what shapes societies. Ultimately, it is about people: How they behave, how they interact with one another, how they organize themselves, what they aspire to. To understand how a society works, we need to understand its people. Around the world, people think and behave differently, the result of the different values they identify with.

Values

In December 2020, we published *Values at the Core: How Human Values Contribute to the Rise of Nations*. We identified four human values that we believe have the strongest impact on economic outcomes: hard work, thrift, trust, and risk-taking.

We argue that some societies, on average, value work more than others, such as historically Protestant (northern Europe, Canada, the US, Australia, New Zealand), Confucian (East Asia), Jewish, and Indian societies. This is not meant to be an exhaustive list. Thousands of ethnic groups exist throughout the world, each with their own values. As we will see in the case of Nigeria, the Igbo are one such group that places heavy emphasis on a strong work ethic and material success.

Hard work is difficult to measure. This has given rise to various controversies, as we will see later on. One way to assess hard work is to look at migrating communities, those who have moved to another country and have done well for themselves wherever they have relocated, irrespective of their initial level of wealth, income, or education. We cannot think of a single example of Chinese, Korean, Japanese, Jewish, Indian, Nigerian Igbo, or Protestant communities relocating to other shores and not becoming as successful (and in many cases, more successful) as other communities, despite the heavy discrimination they often face. Migrants[a] who are already better educated or earn a higher income than the average worker tell us very little about whether their continued success is the result of their values or because of other factors,

---

[a] Throughout this book, we refer to migrants as persons who move from one place to another for an extended period of time.

such as coming from a wealthy family or access to better schools. But if migrants arrive penniless and uneducated and *yet* systematically rise through the ranks everywhere they immigrate to, this to us is clear evidence of the power of human values in changing their economic destiny.

This does not necessarily imply that nations with hardworking citizens will always have better economic prospects. China and India were poor during most of the twentieth century. North Korea seems like a lost cause despite the Confucian influence on its population. For a nation to prosper, the right incentives will need to be in place for people's hard work to be rewarded; that typically takes the form of a market economy.

Thrift is closely related to hard work: Most people who work hard will want to do so to accumulate wealth, but not always. In the US and the UK, traditionally considered as hardworking because of a historically Protestant work ethic, thrift has declined over the years with the rise of consumerism and instant gratification. Just like hard work, thrift is difficult to measure. High personal savings rates do not necessarily imply a thrifty population. People who save a large portion of their income may do so for several reasons: age, income, wealth, family size, the state of the economy, social security, taxes, inflation, interest rates, or education levels. Thrift is rarely considered a factor. Yet, personal savings rates have been consistently high across Confucian and historically Protestant societies (with the recent exception of the US and the UK) for those who have the *ability* to save more. The persistently high personal savings rates of migrants from Confucian and historically Protestant nations, even for second- or third-generation migrants, tell us that thrift does remain ingrained in people, even though they are subject to the same economic factors as the local population in the country where they have resettled.[1]

Trust in others and in political institutions can shape how an economy is structured. Higher trust reduces transaction costs, whereas low trust increases corruption and inequalities. Governments in Nordic countries, where most people trust others and their institutions, are seen as a legitimate distributor of wealth, collecting tax revenues and distributing benefits on a scale much larger than anywhere else, making their societies more equal. Few Scandinavians will try to abuse the system. But applying the same mechanism of high taxes and high distributions to countries where people do not trust each other or their institutions will yield disappointing results. Trust has also played a role in the recent pandemic. Nations with high levels of trust have been much more successful in their fight against COVID-19 with higher vaccination rates and fewer cases and deaths. Nations with low levels of trust, both rich and poor, have struggled with higher mortality rates, even when enforcing strict measures against the virus.[2]

As for risk-taking, taking a lot of risks may be unwise, but minimizing risks in all circumstances can also be detrimental to an economy, preventing households from spending their income, banks from lending, companies from investing and hiring, and entrepreneurs from innovating. Risk-taking tends to be cyclical: People are more likely to take risks when the economy is doing well and become more risk-averse during a downturn. But people in some nations are on average more risk-averse than others. According to surveys, Japan is by far the most risk-averse nation on earth, which in our view is the main reason for its current economic predicament. The citizens of other countries such as Sweden and South Korea are much more willing to take risks, contributing to a more entrepreneurial and innovative culture. In the US, more than a third of Korean migrants have set up their own company, more so than any other ethnic group.[3]

Policies

Values shape societies, but *policies* matter just as much. To function properly, a society requires a set of policies to guide decisions that determine a course of action for the collectivity. In *Values at the Core*, we identified six policies that we believe are the most conducive to prosperity: political stability, free markets, good education, the absence of corruption, and sound fiscal and monetary policies.

Political instability, especially when it manifests itself in the form of war or military coups, is never conducive to growth. Several countries have been locked in a vicious cycle of violence for several decades, with seemingly no end in sight. Sudan, Syria, and Afghanistan have seen almost continuous conflicts since World War II, with devastating effects on the livelihoods of their people. Political stability can be achieved under both authoritarian and democratic regimes. From a purely economic perspective, political stability matters much more than any form of governance.

Free trade *within a nation's domestic market* has proven to be the best way to allocate resources, foster innovative ideas, and create wealth. What we mean by "free markets" is a market-based system where profit-seeking companies operate in a free and fair competitive framework, where new companies are able to enter markets, and where the rule of law allows for strong property rights and contract enforcement. But we are not market fundamentalists. We do not advocate for the role of the state to be minimized at all costs. Public companies can play a very useful role alongside private ones. Too often though, state companies are inefficient and crowd out private ones, preventing them from operating to their full potential. We also make a clear distinction between market forces and the role of the state in redistributing wealth. Both can (and probably should) coexist, as we will see in the case of Sweden.

Those in favor of domestic free trade are often ideologically inclined to support free trade *with other nations*. But there is a fundamental difference between the two. Whereas participants of a domestic free trade framework are, by and large, governed by the same set of national laws, market participants from other countries have to comply with their own sets of rules and regulations which can benefit or hinder their ability to compete on the global stage. A topic of intense debate in recent years, international free trade has seen mixed results. For poor countries that are able to competitively export their products or services, international trade has undeniably been good for them. Others, however, have struggled to compete with cheaper or better-quality imports. As for rich countries, their populations have overall benefited from global trade through lower consumer prices and the global expansion of their firms, yet lower-income groups have at times struggled with increased international competition for their jobs.

In our globalized and highly technological world, education levels are becoming ever more relevant, in rich and poor countries alike. To varying extents, countries are witnessing the offshoring, outsourcing, and automation of many jobs that require fewer qualifications. As modern societies focus increasingly on high-value products and services, workers who lack the required skills are at risk of being left behind. Lifelong learning or re-skilling can help and should be actively pursued, but this will not work for everyone.

While corruption can take place in both public and private sectors, it tends to be more prevalent in the public sector and is clearly damaging to economic growth and society in general. Once corruption becomes endemic, stamping it out becomes very difficult. We argue that a combination of four measures is required to effectively fight corruption: a real willingness and ability from political leaders to fight corruption; an effective rule of law with an independent anti-corruption agency and severe penalties handed out to those found guilty; providing credible alternatives to bribes and other forms of corruption, such as competitive levels of income; and high transparency.

Inequality of both income and wealth has become a pressing issue of our times. Most countries have witnessed rising inequalities over the past 50 years, creating a sense of unfairness among many, and in some cases leading to unrest. The less people trust each other, the wider the inequalities (this becomes a vicious cycle where higher inequalities further reduce levels of trust). Reducing inequalities can be done through global tax treaties. Another option is the adoption of conditional cash transfers, mostly implemented in Latin America and aimed at low-income families, which have reduced inequalities in a region where trust levels are among the lowest in the world.

Price stability constitutes the main mandate given to central banks to conduct monetary policy. High inflation distorts prices, creates confusion, and, if left unchecked, feeds on itself in ever-increasing numbers. Closely associated with the inflation rate, the unemployment rate is the primary indicator to assess trends in the labor market. With the rise of the gig economy, this indicator is in need of reinterpretation as the unemployment rate in many countries hits historical lows. Very low unemployment figures are not necessarily a sign of a booming economy or a sign that there are plenty of *good* jobs available. It should not be an automatic trigger to restrict the money supply; doing so would merely prevent economies from reaching their full potential.

Pitfalls

By associating certain human values with different countries or communities, we are treading a delicate line between two opposing views or interpretations. One is to stereotype, by making statements about certain populations based on anecdotal observation or existing beliefs. As humans, we use mental shortcuts to make sense of the complexity around us, but this can lead to dangerous conclusions. Victims of stereotypes are often thrown into a vicious cycle from which it is difficult to emerge. As French economist Jean Tirole put it, "An individual has weak incentives to behave well if his community has a bad reputation, because he will not be trusted by others anyway and therefore will have fewer opportunities to interact with — and less incentive to develop a good reputation among — those outside his community. In turn, this rational behavior by the individual reinforces others' prejudices regarding the group and contributes to its negative stereotype."[4]

An alternative view is to believe that everyone everywhere has the exact same values that guide their behavior. That people are no more hardworking, thrifty, trusting, or risk-taking in one country or community than any other. Or, if there are differences in values at the individual level, those differences somehow even out at the societal level.

We believe both views to be incorrect. We should recognize that in every society, an entire spectrum of values exists. Each individual is different. But it is our firm belief that certain values are, *on average*, more prevalent in some societies compared to others. In fact, we know this is true for trust and risk-taking, because we are able to measure those values with reasonable precision, through the use of surveys and experiments. We know that people in certain societies, on average, are more trusting and will take on more risk than others.

Hard work and thrift are more difficult to measure. Thrift is not controversial because an absence of thrift is rarely seen in a negative light. But a lack of hard work is often viewed poorly, making discussions around hard work much more sensitive. Most of us will accept that in a classroom, some students work harder than others. In an office or a factory, some employees work harder than others. But when we apply the same logic to an entire society, such observations may sit uncomfortably.

We hope that the arguments put forth in this book will convince readers that there are indeed societies where people, on average, work harder and are more thrifty than others, and that those differences help to shape the way societies have evolved and will continue to evolve. But we need to be mindful not to fall into stereotypes. Tackling those issues requires that we exercise great care and not fall for simplistic explanations.

Overachievers

In the US educational system, Asian Americans consistently outperform other ethnic groups. In 2022, 59% of them earned a bachelor's degree, compared to 42% for Whites, 28% for Blacks and 21% for Hispanics.[5] The cliché of the overachieving Asian student is not just a cliché or a stereotype; it is a fact, evidenced by countless studies that have consistently proven it to be correct.

The data hides another fact: Asian Americans form a very diverse group. The Chinese, Korean, Japanese, Vietnamese all outperform at school, but Americans of Cambodian, Laotian or Filipino ancestry have lower education levels compared to many other groups, including Whites.[6]

Many different factors could explain why East Asians, on average, do so well at schools and universities. One is their socioeconomic background: If their parents earn a high income, if they are highly educated, or if they live in proximity to good schools, those students should do better at school. About three quarters of Asian Americans above 18 years of age were born abroad, many of them already well educated; second- or third-generation migrants to the US often represent the intellectual (and sometimes financial) elite of their country of origin.[7] But, that is not the whole story, because East Asians, on average, do well at school *regardless* of their parents' income level. Students of Vietnamese origin, despite being on average poorer than Whites and many other ethnic groups, still perform better academically than their native-born, middle-class White peers.[8] Other factors that could explain the overall education success of East Asians could be a stronger emphasis on education or a more stable family structure.[9]

Then there is hard work, which we believe is a big factor in explaining those differences. Around 93 percent of Asian Americans view people in their country of origin as very hardworking, compared to 57 percent of Asian Americans who describe the American population as such.[10] East Asians in the US are more likely than others to believe that academic achievement results from greater effort, rather than greater skill.[11] They believe that hard work pays off and they will therefore be incentivized to work harder. A familiar pattern is that of a first generation of migrants with little education struggling to make a living but ensuring that their children get the best possible education; the second generation is often much more successful, working hard to make the most of the education they received and to make their parents proud. This is likely to be greatly advantageous to them for the rest of their lives: in the US, Asian Americans are better paid than Whites, their application for mortgages are nearly twice as likely to be successful compared to Whites and Asian American employees are less likely to be let go from their job than their White counterparts.[12] Do those observations mean that White Americans are discriminated against Asian Americans? Not at all. It simply reflects the fact that on average, Asian Americans are higher achievers.

Beyond discrimination

If certain minorities such as East Asians tend to be more highly educated and earn a higher income, other minorities struggle with lower income and lower educational levels. This is the case for Black Americans (we focus once again on the US given the available data, but our observations are likely to apply to other countries as well). Over the past 20 years, the income levels of Black Americans have hardly increased, even before COVID-19.[13] The COVID-19 pandemic has taken its greatest economic toll on Black communities, who are more likely to have lost their job or fallen behind in paying their bills.[14] On average, Blacks earn less than Hispanics, Whites, or Asians.

One reason is that Blacks are discriminated against. Several studies have shown that Blacks have more difficulties securing well-paying jobs compared to other applicants with similar qualifications. They are more likely to face bullying at school or at the workplace, to be the victims of crimes, to be arrested, and to serve longer sentences for the same crimes. Recent cases of police brutality have been a painful reminder of the difficulties faced by Blacks, in the US and elsewhere.

It would, however, be a mistake to conclude that discrimination is the *only* reason why certain minorities earn less and struggle academically.

Similar to how different groups of Asian Americans end up with different educational and income levels, the same holds true for Black Americans. Foreign-born Black migrants earn about 20 percent more than native-born Blacks. That in itself is not surprising. Many of those coming to the US are highly educated, and, in some cases, already wealthy. Many are seeking better opportunities rather than fleeing poverty or conflicts. This gap between native-born and immigrant Blacks is unlikely to be caused by human values or any other cultural factor.[15]

Yet, large differences in income levels remain persistent between Black communities. The median household income for Nigerian Americans is 40 percent higher than that of other Black Americans. Nigerian Americans earn almost double as much as Americans from Ethiopia or the Dominican Republic.[16] Why would Nigerian migrants be so much more successful than other Black migrants? Surely they are not less discriminated against. Many of them arrived penniless to the US following the Nigerian Civil War in the late 1960s, as we will see later in this book. And yet, over time, they have become one of the most successful US minorities. More than 20 percent of Black students at Harvard Business School are of Nigerian ancestry, even though they make up just one percent of Blacks in the country.[17]

Racial discrimination has been detrimental to Nigerians in the US and elsewhere, but it never stopped them from achieving economic success. Other minorities have also done well for themselves despite being heavily discriminated against, such as the Chinese in Malaysia, the Indians in East Africa, or the Jews in Russia. Discrimination is a serious and unjustifiable societal scourge that must be addressed and opposed, but it is not the sole explanation for the very different economic outcomes of those communities. Our contention is that values play a crucial role in how each community and country develops and prospers. In the words of economist Thomas Sowell: In many countries around the world, the abandoning or discrediting of the concept of achievement leads to blaming higher achieving groups for the fact that other groups are lower achievers, putting many societies on the road to racial and ethnic polarization, and sometimes on the road to ruin.[18]

We should be mindful never to label one society as superior to another because their people identify more strongly with certain values compared to other societies. Some communities will value materialistic gains and the efforts required to achieve those gains, more than others. This is likely to lead to higher standards of living, longer life expectancy, more purchasing power, and better healthcare. But it may also lead to a more competitive and individualistic society, higher stress levels and suicide rates, declining birth rates, and weaker family ties. As we will see in the chapter on Oman, working more to achieve higher wealth may not necessarily make people happier. Ultimately, the short amount of time that we spend on this planet should be about living a happy and fulfilling life, with each of us having a different perspective on what that means and how to achieve it.

A world of values

In this book, we apply these concepts to twelve different countries spread across five continents. The countries were selected not only for their contribution to the world economy but also because they illustrate how values and policies interact. The chapters devoted to each country have been arranged in no particular order and can therefore be read independently. They are not meant to be exhaustive: An entire book could have been devoted to each country. But we have tried, within the few pages devoted to each country, to present how the combination of values and policies has led to where each country stands today and where it might be headed going forward.

We begin with Brazil, known not only for its sandy beaches, soccer team, and warm-hearted people but also for its long periods of economic stagnation and the wide gap between the rich and the poor. Next up is Singapore, which moved from third world to sprawling metropolis in just a generation, a model of policymaking built on the foundation of a hardworking and thrifty population. The Nordic or Scandinavian model, arguably the best economic model ever conceived, is often misunderstood as a socialist one. We focus on Sweden and stress the importance of trust in others and in public institutions. We then move to Botswana, a rare African success story that made tremendous progress since gaining independence, largely as a result of its ability to capitalize on abundant natural resources and the vision of one man. Next is India, which has become a major economy since embarking on much-needed reforms in the early 1990s. It has, however, for a long time been growing more slowly than China, hampered by excessive regulations.

After 40 years of post-war prosperity, Japan has struggled with anemic growth. A series of bold experiments in the past decade have yielded some result, but not to the extent hoped for by policymakers. The largest economy in Africa, Nigeria is an oil-rich and ethnically diverse nation, composed of three major ethnic groups, each with a different set of values and struggling at times to get along with each other. The US remains the biggest and one of the most innovative economies in the world, achieving prosperity through its adherence to free markets and individual liberties as well as a historical desire to work hard and accumulate wealth. The country has, however, become increasingly polarized and unequal, leading some of those who have been left behind to question its model. Greece endured a traumatic crisis in the wake of the Great Recession, forced to implement much-hated reforms. We argue that a Nordic model of high taxes and distributions will not work for Greece, given the lack of trust Greeks have for each other or their political institutions.

China has been the biggest success story of the past 30 years, lifting millions out of poverty. No country can ignore its growing influence, which is met with excitement by some and apprehension by others. As living standards improve, the necessary transition from savings and exports to a more consumerist and innovative society is well under way; but this also comes with its own set of challenges. After the fall of the Soviet Union, Russia endured a chaotic decade in the 1990s before achieving much-needed stability and sustained growth. Yet, the economy has never really recovered since 2009, as private companies struggle to compete against state giants and rampant corruption. We conclude with Oman, a small Arab state reliant on oil and a foreign workforce, like most of its neighbors. Omanis are generally content with the life they have, grateful to their leaders for the way they have managed the country's oil wealth. But they are at risk of seeing their livelihoods severely affected as and when oil revenues run out.

Chapter 1

Brazil

C arnival holds a special place in the heart of most Brazilians. The 5-day extravaganza historically marked the beginning of Lent, the period of 40 days before Easter during which Roman Catholics abstain from consuming meat ("carnival" comes from the Latin *carne levare,* "to remove meat"). While Carnival is celebrated in many other countries, Brazilians take it to another level. Rio de Janeiro, the city that attracts the most participants, sees six million locals and tourists take to the streets every year in what is considered the biggest party on Earth.

Carnival is a celebration of life and happiness where social conventions are turned upside down, allowing Brazilians to escape their daily grind. It sets them free, if only for a few days — free to ridicule almost anything and anyone in a society that remains conservative and hierarchical. It is also a time of unity in a divided nation, where those of different regions, social backgrounds, and races come together to drink, dance, and party. The various cultural influences of Brazil (mainly indigenous, European, and Afro-Brazilian) feature prominently in the costumes, dances, and music.

Carnival in Brazil is always an extravagant affair. Yet, some years are more extravagant than others, offering a glimpse into the prevailing mood of the country. In recent years, celebrations have been more muted.

Festivities in some cities have been toned down or cancelled altogether. Budgets have been cut. Companies that, only a decade ago, were competing against each other to secure the best sponsoring deals have been conspicuous by their absence. Street parties with their own musical bands, known as *blocos*, are replacing the more traditional and expensive parades, for which samba schools prepare all year round. Rio had 500 blocos in 2023 compared to 300 in 2007.[1] Participants are less willing to spend at the parades, preferring instead to attend the free blocos. Samba schools are struggling to secure financial support after public funding was cut in recent years.[2] The number of floats, dancers, and musicians have all been reduced. Even the bird wings that adorn many costumes, traditionally made from real feathers, have at times been replaced by painted, plastic replicas. The 2021 and 2022 editions, which had to be cancelled because of the pandemic, had left a void for many in Brazil.

Fifteen years ago, things looked very different. Back then, as Brazil was gearing up to organize the soccer World Cup and the Olympics, Rio's official samba stadium, the Sambadrome, was renovated and expanded at a cost of US$20 million. Next to the Sambadrome, an open-air space was overhauled for another US$9 million.[3] Spectators were at times paying thousands of dollars to secure the best seats at the parades. Those were the days of unlimited budgets and endless expectations.

Carnival will remain a quintessential expression of Brazilian culture for many years to come. But will the celebrations ever be as wild as they were a decade ago?

A few booms and many busts

Every country goes through periods of growth and slowdown. But in Brazil, the eighth most populous nation in the world, strong growth has been a rarity, almost an anomaly. Throughout the country's modern history, most Brazilians have had little to cheer for on the economic front.

Stagnating incomes and fast-rising prices have been the norm during most of their lives.

Long periods of slumber have been intertwined with rare decades of prosperity. Brazilians are so used to bad economic news that when the good times do come, they are seen as "miracles" or "magic moments." After a few years of prosperity, the mood switches completely, from unbridled pessimism to excessive optimism. People become convinced that Brazil is destined for greatness, that good times will last forever. When the crisis hits, as it inevitably does, it is met with disbelief and the slow realization that the country is back to its old ways.

Brazil enjoyed two significant spells of strong growth. The first one took place in the late 1960s and early 1970s. In 1964, a military dictatorship took over in a coup, remaining in power for more than 20 years. The dictatorship's legacy is highly controversial: Thousands of political dissidents were tortured and hundreds murdered. But the absence of democracy was never an impediment to Brazil's economic growth. In fact, the dictatorship brought much needed stability after years of political uncertainty in the early 1960s. Military leaders had little understanding or interest in running the economy, delegating that responsibility to a group that became known as the "technocrats."

The technocrats made three important decisions. The first was to tackle hyperinflation. This was done by raising interest rates and led to 3 years of hardship from 1964 to 1967, but brought inflation under control and paved the way for much faster growth from 1968 onward. The second decision was to open Brazil to the world. Exports became more diversified: Whereas the country used to sell mostly coffee outside its borders, it began to export more sugar, soybeans, and manufactured goods. Exports procedures were simplified, export taxes abolished, export subsidies put in place, and the local currency devalued. The third decision was to spend freely: Big investments were made on infrastructure, modernizing the country's massive road network and engaging in large-scale projects.

The results exceeded most expectations. Brazil became an industrialized nation, transitioning from a predominantly agricultural society to a manufacturing one. Millions of people moved from the countryside into cities. Production of iron and steel, electric power, passenger cars, and household appliances reached record highs. Foreign companies set up factories in the country. GDP grew by ten percent annually over a decade.[4]

But in the mid-1970s, the economy unraveled. Market forces remained shackled by the state, offering few opportunities for private companies to grow and innovate. Government expenses became increasingly financed by foreign loans. Brazil's growing external debt had become a burden in the late 1970s and early 1980s as global interest rates surged. The international oil shocks further strained the country's finances: Brazil was not yet a large oil producer and therefore had to purchase most of its oil from abroad. Domestic interest rates had been reduced significantly even during the good years, allowing inflation to make a comeback. Most prices, wages, exchange rates, and even taxes were indexed to inflation, further fueling an inflationary spiral. Prices more than doubled every year in the 1980s till the mid-1990s. Brazil never had an independent central bank. The political leaders who managed monetary policy had been unwilling to raise interest rates and incur the wrath of their citizens.

Brazilians had to wait until the late 1990s for hyperinflation to finally be defeated. A new currency, the real, was introduced and interest rates were once again raised sharply. Ironically, rates were increased not so much to fight inflation, but in a failed attempt to preserve the value of the real as foreign investors were taking their money elsewhere. Predictably, higher interest rates led to another recession in 1998, but also paved the way for a new economic miracle. This time, the state retreated: Several rounds of privatizations took place in the 1990s and early 2000s, improving the efficiency of Brazilian companies.

The second spell of strong growth started in the early 2000s. It was feared that, as a former union leader, President Luiz Inácio Lula da Silva, better known as Lula, would nationalize companies and impose heavy regulations. He did not. His policies were very much a continuation of what his predecessor had put in place. But they also coincided with a commodity super-cycle that lasted more than a decade. Much of what China required to power its economy was produced in Brazil: iron ore, soybeans, sugar, and oil. Brazil's economy has always been heavily reliant on commodities, which account for about 65 percent of exports and 15 percent of Gross Domestic Product or GDP.[5] Exports doubled from 1999 to 2004.[6] Foreign investors were back, keen to get involved once again. With so much money flowing in, a good portion of Brazil's foreign debt was repaid (including that of the much-despised IMF) and public spending surged, mostly on infrastructure and social programs. As interest rates were kept high, inflation continued to recede to around five percent, the lowest rate in more than 50 years.

But as commodity prices declined in the early 2010s and the rest of the world struggled in the aftermath of the 2008 financial crisis, so did Brazil. Exports crumbled. Similar to what happened in the late 1970s, foreign investors, realizing that the party was over, exited in droves. Most of them had come for a quick profit, not for long-term investments in new factories or other job-creating ventures. With less money flowing in, spending cuts became necessary. At least global interest rates remained low, enabling Brazil to avoid defaulting on its foreign debt.

Tropical languor

The unfortunate reality is that the few periods of fast growth that Brazil enjoyed were never going to last forever because they relied on factors that are not sustainable over time: population growth, commodity prices, foreign investments, and large public spending. For growth to be sustained, it needs to be the result of improvements in productivity. Between 1990 and 2012, labor productivity accounted for just 40 percent of Brazil's GDP growth, compared with 91 percent in China and 67 percent in India.[7] China and India did start from a much lower base in 1990 compared to Brazil, but the fact that most of their GDP growth is the result of higher labor productivity tells us that their growth is more sustainable over time.

Brazil's inability to generate long-lasting growth and higher living standards has a lot to do with the work ethic of its population. One of the most iconic books written about Brazilian society, one that most Brazilians will be familiar with, is *Roots of Brazil*, written in 1936 by historian and sociologist Sérgio Buarque de Holanda.[8] The book aims to describe the essence of what it means to be Brazilian, inventing the concept of the "cordial man," a person guided by the heart (*cor* means heart in Latin), for whom emotions triumph over reason. Holanda attributes this concept to the Portuguese and Spanish influence, the rural–urban divide, and the strong family ties that form an essential part of Brazilian society.

Comparing the different waves of migration to the Americas, Holanda differentiates between "workers" and "adventurers." The workers, who colonized the United States and Canada, were raised with a Protestant work ethic. They value security, effort, and long-term rewards. The adventurers are the Portuguese and the Spanish, who colonized Brazil and the rest of Latin America. Adventurers ignore constraints and "do not appreciate the virtues of dreary effort. Their ideal is to pick the fruit without planting the tree." According to Holanda, "The modern religion of work and appreciation for utilitarian activity never became part of the Hispanics peoples' nature. To a good Portuguese or to a Spaniard, a dignified idleness always seemed more desirable and also more ennobling than the insane struggle for daily bread. Both idealize the effortless and unconcerned life of a grandee. Thus, while the Protestant peoples praise and glorify manual labor, the Iberian nations still see things more from the viewpoint of classical antiquity. The older concepts — that leisure is worth more than business, and that productive activity is in itself less valuable than contemplation and love — are dominant among them. Among the Spanish and Portuguese, a strong work ethic was always an exotic fruit."

Holanda also describes how slavery further diminished the incentive to work. Brazil imported more than 5 million slaves, mostly from Africa, and was the last nation to abolish slavery in 1888. Slavery fulfilled the need for labor, enabling the Portuguese colonizers to search for easy riches without having to do much work. "Slavery heightened the effect of elements conspiring against the spirit of work by killing the need for the free man to cooperate and organize." Adalberto Cardoso, a professor of sociology in Rio de Janeiro, further notes that "The legacy of slavery crystallized an ethics that devalues manual labor, deeming it unworthy, unclean and derogatory."[9]

This desire for effortless prosperity still resonates today. At the beginning of the twentieth century, Japanese migrants arrived in Brazil destitute and uneducated, yet they gradually climbed the social ladder through their hard work despite heavy discrimination, ultimately becoming one of the highest-income communities in the country, ahead of White Brazilians. As fellow disciples of a Confucian work ethic, Chinese companies with operations in the country, forced by law to hire locals instead of importing their own workforce, often complain about what they perceive to be the lax work ethic of Brazilian employees.[10] This negative attitude toward work may be an overgeneralization, but it is preventing the country's economy from joining the ranks of highly industrialized nations.

Car washing

Another human value in short supply is social trust. Latin America is the region with the lowest levels of social trust in the world. Only seven percent of Brazilians trust each other. Even in 2010, when the country was highly prosperous, the proportion never exceeded 10 percent.[11] Around 80 percent of Brazilians believe that others want to take advantage of them in some way.[12]

Corruption thrives when people do not trust each other. It is endemic in Brazil, affecting all sectors. Because personal relationships are highly valued (a throwback to Holanda's "cordial man"), the line between public and private is often blurred. Bribes are not uncommon in conducting business, whether this relates to government contracts, speeding up paperwork, obtaining a driving license, or seeking other favors. In an effort to hide their identity, people or companies sometimes resort to front men, known locally as *testa de ferro* or *laranja*, to conduct fraudulent transactions such as tax evasion or bribery.

Brazilian bureaucracy is as old as the country itself. A Ministry of Debureaucratization was even set up in 1979. Despite some early success, it was dissolved less than a decade later. Excessive bureaucracy creates a fertile environment for corruption. Most people are forced to spend hours filling out endless forms and waiting in line. The most privileged will use *despachante*, people with the right connections who will help them navigate the bureaucracy for a fee. Bribes are sometimes involved, but patience and creative thinking are the main skills required.

Many Brazilians have understandably lost hope that things will ever change. A popular local expression is *Rouba mas faz*: He steals, but he gets things done. When Eike Batista, Brazil's richest man in the early 2010s, was put on trial in 2015 for insider trading, the judge presiding over his case had ordered several of his assets to be impounded. A few days later, the same judge was seen driving one of the impounded cars, a Porsche Cayenne; he had also put Batista's piano in a neighbor's apartment.[13] Brazil ranks 94th out of the 180 countries in Transparency International's Corruptions Perceptions Index (CPI). Many other Latin America countries fare no better: Colombia ranks 91st, Argentina 94th, Peru 101st, and Mexico 126th.[14]

Cracking down on corruption once it has become endemic, in countries with very low social trust, is very challenging. It takes time to change mentalities. But it is not impossible. Uruguay and Chile, ranked 14th and 27th, respectively, on the CPI list, provide evidence that corruption in Latin America can be maintained at relatively low levels. Bureaucracy needs to be reduced, perpetrators brought to justice, and strong punishments handed out. Operation Car Wash, which unveiled massive corruption in 2019, put behind bars powerful figures of industry and politics, something that was unimaginable only a few years earlier. This may be a sign that things are changing. But if they are, this will be a very gradual process; it will probably require a new generation for mentalities to truly evolve.

Bolsa Família

Much like the rest of Latin America, Brazil is a very unequal society, another consequence of very low trust levels. The contrast is stark between wealthy families that dominate the corporate landscape and those struggling to feed their families, in the countryside and in *favelas,* the impoverished neighborhoods of larger cities.

There was, however, one major difference between the growth spells of the early 1970s and the 2000s: Whereas the economic boom of the early 1970s mostly benefited already wealthy Brazilians, the one in the 2000s lifted millions out of poverty. The greatest legacy of Lula's first term in office has been *Bolsa Família* ("family allowance"), a conditional cash transfer (CCT) program that provides cash handouts to low-income families as long as they satisfy certain conditions, such as ensuring that their children regularly attend school and are vaccinated, as well as regular visits to a doctor for pregnant or breastfeeding mothers. The program was first put in place by Lula's predecessor, but it was greatly expanded and enhanced under Lula. Over time, it has become the largest CCT program in the world, covering a quarter of Brazil's population.

Because the cash transfers are conditional, they provide a higher incentive for families to send their kids to school and spend more on medicine and food.[15] Cash is usually given to women, who tend to spend it more wisely than men. Each eligible beneficiary receives a debit card to withdraw the funds once a month from a government-owned bank; this is much preferable to relying on local officials to distribute the funds, as they may withhold them or insist on a bribe. The amounts given are relatively low (around $120 per month), but they make a world of difference to impoverished families, some of whom earn less than $1 a day.

The results have been spectacular. 30 million poor Brazilians have been lifted out of poverty, joining the ranks of the middle class (defined in Brazil as individuals with an income of between $150 and $500 per month). Most of the funds received are spent on food, followed by school supplies and clothing.[16] Children eat better, receiving free meals when they attend public schools. School grades have improved, though mostly among girls.[17] Children are less likely to be involved in child labor and even grow taller more quickly than they did before the program was put in place.[18]

Inequalities have declined, as they did in every Latin American country that implemented CCTs. This is a remarkable achievement in a world where inequalities have increased. The income of the poorest 10 percent of Brazilians grew by about 9 percent per year between 2001 and 2006, compared with 2–4 percent for the richest people.[19] The GINI coefficient, a measure of inequality, gradually declined from 2001 to 2009, although it remains high by international standards.[20]

The costs related to Bolsa Família have stayed low, representing less than 0.5 percent of the GDP.[21] Yet, in the years prior to the COVID-19 pandemic, cuts were made. Fewer families are eligible. Given the clear benefits of the program, a major rollback would reverse years of social progress. This is unlikely to happen, at least for now: The program is being revived (and expanded) under Lula's third term as president.

Trapped

Despite temporary bursts of strong growth, Brazil remains stuck as a middle-income country. Its GDP per capita, hovering around US$10,000, represents just a fraction of what countries such as South Korea have achieved, despite starting at the same level in the early 1960s.

Policy improvements have been made. The country struggled with high inflation for decades until it was defeated in the mid-1990s. It may still come back, but a well-calibrated monetary policy should prevent it (it currently stands at a very respectable 5 percent). Things could be worse: Neighboring Argentina continues to grapple with very high inflation rates (currently at more than 100 percent), preventing any meaningful progress. Bolsa Família has been a resounding success in reducing inequalities. As a middle-income nation, Brazil has benefited from globalization, selling its products around the world.

The country has room for further improvement. Little has been done so far to instill more market forces into Brazil's domestic market. Too many industries are run by family-owned monopolies, reducing their incentive to become more efficient. Competition is weak and obstructed by corrupt practices. Doing business in Brazil remains very challenging. In its Ease of Doing Business index, the World Bank ranks Brazil 124th, a ranking that has not improved in the past 20 years. As a telling example, and although Brazil and Mexico have a similar GDP per capita, selling a Mexican-made car in Brazil is 12 percent cheaper for an automaker than selling a locally made vehicle, including production, tax, and logistics costs.[22] Starting a new business in Brazil is an uphill battle: On average, it takes 13 procedures and 119 days of work. Construction permits demand an average of 17 procedures and 469 days to finally get authorized.[23] The judiciary continues to be hampered by delays, corruption, nepotism, and politicization.

Reforms to make Brazil's economy more dynamic, by slashing bureaucracy, cracking down on corruption, and ensuring free and fair competition, would certainly lead to improvements. But those reforms will not be sufficient to allow Brazil to extirpate itself from the middle-income trap. At best, it could achieve what Chile has achieved, with a GDP per capita of around $15,000. It is often said that Brazil is the country of the future; its people know full well that it always will be. Then again, for Holanda's "adventurers," while materialistic gains are desirable, priorities in life also lie elsewhere. Brazilians are rightly proud of a nation that evokes images of "unspoiled and exquisitely beautiful scenery, leafy indolence, sensuality, humor, cordiality, equatorial legend and racial harmony," as one journalist once put it.[24] Those features may not be quantifiable, but they form an essential part of Brazil's identity and contribute just as much to the well-being of its people.

Chapter 2

Singapore

O n 12 November 1978, Lee Kuan Yew, Singapore's prime minister since the island-state acquired its independence in 1965, was waiting on the runway of Paya Lebar airport, eager for his visitor to arrive. The plane soon landed and Deng Xiaoping emerged from it, accompanied by a 36-strong delegation. He walked down the flight of stairs and shook hands with Lee, both men smiling and keen to get started. Deng Xiaoping was second-in-command in the Chinese political hierarchy and making his first official visit to Singapore.[1]

The two men had great admiration for each other and would spend the next 2 days in discussions. Politics was on the agenda, including the Soviet Union and Vietnam, which at the time had views to expand militarily in the region. But Deng was also very curious about Singapore's economic model. At first glance, the two nations had little in common: Singapore was a tiny country of less than 3 million inhabitants, mostly working in manufacturing and services, whereas China's population of almost a billion people was mainly employed in agriculture.

Deng was impressed by what he saw. The city was clean and modern, with new buildings erected seemingly everywhere. Its economy, vibrant and opened to the world, attracted many foreign companies and was becoming a global leader in industries, such as container shipping, electronics, and finance. Its workforce was well educated and able to hold its own against foreign competition. The country's unique public housing program that allowed households to acquire a property at below-market price was clearly successful with a majority of Singaporeans living in public housing estates. Here was a nation with a Chinese majority and an authoritarian leadership that had somehow achieved a spectacular level of development. If descendants of Chinese laborers could achieve such a feat, what was to stop China from doing the same?

Not long after his visit to Singapore, Deng became China's paramount leader. He instituted reforms that, to a large extent, replicated the policies put in place by Singapore, heralding his country's own economic miracle. Over the years that followed, thousands of Chinese officials visited Singapore to learn about its policies and corporate management methods.

How did Singapore manage such fast and sustained growth, becoming one of the most developed economies in the world, progressing from third to first world, transforming itself from a port town into a sprawling metropolis within a generation? This was achieved through sound economic policies: free markets, political stability, excellent education, low corruption, and sound fiscal and monetary policies. But economic policies alone would not have brought such prosperity to Singapore; the island nation would have progressed, but not to the extent that it did without certain human values conducive to growth.

Competing with the world

Despite western and other influences, Chinese Singaporeans, who make up 70 percent of Singapore's population, have by and large retained their Confucian heritage. One of the values that children in Singapore grow up with is the importance of hard work, a key tenet of Confucian thought. Another value inherited by Singapore citizens is thrift. Similar to other East Asian economies, Singapore saves a large portion of its income, 43 percent of the GDP in 2022, implying that households, businesses, and the state *collectively* save almost half of their income.[2] Corresponding figures for the US or the UK were 18 percent and 16 percent, respectively.

A high savings rate leads to high investments. Singapore has invested massively in its infrastructure: residential estates, office buildings, warehouses, manufacturing plants, seaports, airports, and public transportation. Entire neighborhoods are redesigned and redeveloped on a regular basis. The country has embarked on large-scale land reclamation works since the 1970s and reduced its water dependency on neighboring Malaysia to less than 50 percent of its needs by building reservoirs, barrages, and desalinization plants.

With a thrifty population and a very limited domestic market of just 5 million inhabitants (and less than 2 million at independence), the country had no choice but to open up to the world. This has been achieved on an unprecedented scale: Singapore has the highest trade-to-GDP ratio in the world with imports and exports representing over 3 times what the country produces.[3] The need to embrace international trade was recognized early on by Lee. Despite lacking technical and managerial skills, Singapore did not attempt to protect its infant industries. Lee felt confident that its hardworking population, supported by a small but growing group of highly educated workers and policymakers, would rapidly learn new skills and be able to compete on the international stage, even if that meant being exploited in the beginning: "The prevailing theory then was that multinationals were exploiters of cheap labor and cheap raw materials and would suck a country dry. We had no raw materials for them to exploit. All we had was the labor. Nobody else wanted to exploit the labor. So why not, if they want to exploit our labor? They're welcome to it. And we found that whether or not they exploited us, we were learning how to do a job from them, which we would never have learnt. We were learning on the job and being paid for it."

Lee was also very curious about economies and political systems in other countries, observing what worked and what did not. Just like Deng Xiaoping, he was a pragmatic man who did not care much about ideologies or grand theories. Together with other government members, he experimented with new ideas and concepts on a small scale, proceeding further if the experiments proved successful. Only the results mattered. Sometimes, it ended in failure, for example, when the country ventured into shipbuilding. But instead of clinging on to failed projects, Singapore moved on and specialized in other more promising industries: Today, it is a recognized leader in sectors such as electronics, finance, energy, port containers, chemicals, and biotechnologies, a feat its population could not have achieved if the country had not opened its borders to the world, reducing trade barriers and entering into several free trade agreements.

A model of economic policy

Although Lee considered the merits of a planned economy in his younger days, he quickly came to realize the superior potential for growth that free markets could provide. Singapore is a market economy in which few regulations distort the efficient allocation of resources, providing a free and fair competitive environment for companies to conduct their activities. Most companies can be set up in a matter of hours. Those that have failed will be quickly wound down, not kept artificially alive. This process of creative destruction has allowed the Singapore economy to be regularly ranked among the most competitive in the world.

That is not to say that the government plays no role. Quite the contrary. Hundreds of public companies operate in Singapore, mostly owned by Temasek, a government holding company, making up a third of all market capitalizations.[4] Public companies (or government-linked corporations as they are known locally) were initially set up in the late 1960s to compensate for the lack of private funding and expertise available back then. Creditors were reluctant to lend to new, untested companies without the backing of the state. In many countries, the presence of public companies has stalled economic growth as they often benefit from more favorable funding and accommodative regulations, ultimately making them less competitive compared to private firms, which themselves struggles to become efficient as they are unable to compete on an equal footing. But in Singapore, this model has worked out well, primarily because public companies cannot expect preferential treatment from the government, which does not meddle in their operations. They are subject to the same rules and regulations as private companies and are not to be used for social or employment generation purposes.[5] Many of those companies are listed, further exposing them to market scrutiny and discipline. Public company workers as well as government officials can expect wages similar to those in the private sector. The dominance of large public companies has enabled the country to invest outside its borders, more so than any small or medium-sized company ever could, but it has also reduced the ability of local private firms to compete and grow against these much larger players that do not rely on state support but nevertheless benefit from economies of scale. A balance therefore needs to be struck: A competitive market economy cannot solely comprise large public companies.

Foreign companies are also put on an equal footing with local ones, whether public or private. They are not discriminated against and are not required to involve a local partner as is the case in many other countries in the region. Some have set up factories and regional or global headquarters in Singapore despite the higher operational costs involved. They do so not only because of low corporate taxes and a competent workforce but also because they know that in Singapore *things work*: The system is efficient and the rules are clear.

The country is constantly reinventing itself. Cognizant of the fact that innovation had lagged behind, efforts were made at the turn of the century to foster a more innovative environment and attract techno-logical firms from around the world. Singapore ranks as the fifth most innovative nation in the world according to the Global Innovation Index, an annual ranking that assesses a nation's level of innovation. The country hosts dedicated research hubs in biotechnologies and pharmaceuticals and invests heavily to promote itself as a technology center. There are more than 50 biomedical manufacturing plants in Singapore, employing close to 20,000 workers.[6] Entrepreneurship has also taken off over the past decade. The government supports start-ups by funding them, giving incentives to local banks to invest in them, promoting links with local universities, and acting as an intermediary between start-ups and senior business executives or potential investors. Although it remains a nascent sector, it increasingly contributes to a more innovative society.

This economic dynamism is underpinned by a strong legal frame-work. Companies operate under a clear, credible, and independent legal system that delivers swift dispensation of justice. That was not always the case. In the 1980s, as the number of legal cases increased signifi-cantly, Singapore's judicial system became strained and a backlog of unresolved cases quickly formed. Reforms were implemented in the 1990s under the tenure of Chief Justice Yong Pung How. Legal docu-ments were digitized, allowing for much quicker filing and retrieval. Judges were instructed to avoid time wastage such as when the cross-examination of witnesses was deemed to be irrelevant. Punitive sen-tences were handed out to those deemed guilty of filing frivolous appeals. This is in stark contrast with many other countries where legal decisions can take years before coming into force after endless appeals. Mediation and pre-trial conferences resulted in many cases being resolved before going to trial. As a testament to the quality of its judi-cial system, the island-state has become a center for international arbitration.

Tackling corruption

Upon independence, Lee and his ministers were determined to fight corruption. Lee understood that without the determination of top leaders to eradicate corruption, little would be achieved: "Once a political system has been corrupted right from the very top leaders to the lowest rungs of the bureaucracy, the problem is very complicated. The cleansing and disinfecting has to start from top and go downwards in a thorough and systematic way. It is a long and laborious process that can be carried out only by a very strong group of leaders with the strength and moral authority derived from unquestioned integrity."[7] With a leadership dedicated to tackling corruption, those tasked with implementing policies further down the ranks are selected on merit and paid competitively to reduce the incentive for them to abuse their powers.

Building upon the strong institutions inherited from the British, Singapore enacted several laws to strongly penalize offenders. The burden of proof falls onto the accused, meaning that the person must explain the origin of any wealth that appears disproportionate in relation to known sources of income. Enforceability is not limited to the Singapore territory: Any Singaporean resident can be pursued whether his or her offences are committed in Singapore or abroad. The anti-corruption agency is manned by highly paid and well-educated officials. Over the years, senior ministers and corporate executives have been forced to step down and occasionally jailed when found guilty of corrupt practices. Another factor in reducing corruption has been the crackdown on bureaucracy. Administrative processes are clearly explained and simplified as much as possible. Most government services are available online. Starting a company, applying for licenses, filing taxes, and purchasing property are all straightforward processes that reduce the opportunity for anyone to collect bribes. Of course, the battle against corruption is never truly won. While Singapore has done very well in this domain, it has to remain vigilant as a resurgence of corruption can never be excluded.

Top of the class

As a country devoid of natural resources, Singapore has invested heavily in its most valuable asset: its people. Schools are compulsory and heavily subsidized, underpinned by the meritocratic idea that students should be given equal opportunities in life regardless of their background. Children are not allowed to be enrolled in private schools.[8] The educational system is highly competitive and demanding for all involved: students, parents, tutors, and teachers. Similar to other East Asian societies, the focus is on hard work, with plenty of homework and tutoring classes keeping students busy. But where Singapore differentiates itself from its East Asian counterparts is that after years of focusing on rote learning, efforts have been made in recent years to promote creativity in the classroom in the hope that this will contribute to a more innovative society and equip students with better skills. Exam questions are becoming more open-ended to encourage critical thinking, and courses such as 3D design and robotics have been introduced. A 2015 Programme for International Student Assessment (PISA) ranking on collaborative problem-solving placed Singapore first in the world. The focus remains very much on hard work, with long hours of study and tutoring still the norm. Yet, those long hours do not seem to make students less happy: Overall, Singaporean pupils report themselves to be happier compared to many other countries, including those in Scandinavia where students spend far less time studying.[9]

That said, this highly demanding and competitive environment does put a lot of pressure on students. The uncertainties and restrictions caused by COVID-19 further increased levels of stress, at times leading to despair. In 2022, Singapore reported the highest number of suicides in the past 20 years, with most of those suicides occurring in the 20–29 years age bracket.[10] Such trends are not specific to Singapore, but there has historically been a certain stigma attached to children's and young adult's mental health. Few students confide in parents, teachers, or counselors when faced with mental health issues. Singapore's education system is likely to remain a highly stressful experience for many students.

Another factor leading to Singapore topping global education rankings has been its focus on teachers, setting up a rigorous process of selection, training, and appraisal. Teachers are recruited among top graduates and trained for several months at the National Institute of Education. Continuous learning applies to the teaching profession: Every teacher is required to undergo 100 hours of training *each year* to learn about new pedagogical techniques and professional development. A majority of them feel that their profession is highly valued in society, which is essential to their continued motivation and in attracting top talent.[11] They are, on average, well paid: The starting salary of a secondary school teacher is 30 percent above the national median income.[12] Teachers are regularly appraised on the effectiveness of their teaching. Those who do not perform are required to undergo further professional development; in some cases, they may be let go. Those who outperform are rewarded with monetary gains and promotions. Whenever a teacher is promoted, he or she enters a new salary bracket, giving the person an additional incentive to perform. Since the performance of teachers depends to a large extent on how well their students perform, teachers cannot grade the exams of their own students. Exams are graded by teachers from other schools on an anonymous basis: Exam papers contain a registration number but not the name of the student. The system is not perfect, with teachers occasionally complaining of a high administrative burden and long, stressful hours. But the results are undeniable: Singapore students consistently rank among the highest achievers in international rankings for science, reading, and mathematics.[13] The country's main universities also feature prominently in global rankings.

Subsidized education does not stop at the school or university level. In an effort to equip its citizens with the best possible work qualifications throughout their careers, the country promotes continuous learning, mainly through a program called *SkillsFuture*, which offers more than 10,000 learning courses in various fields at discounted costs and for which each Singaporean is awarded a non-expiring initial credit of about US$350. One of the writers of this book (ChinHwee) co-leads the Alliance for Action on Edutech, a government-sponsored initiative that explores how the use of technology can provide better skills to Singaporeans. One example is a platform that provides personalized career and learning recommendations for workers. In a fast-changing world, people need to upgrade their skills. Employers also play their part, identifying those skills most likely to be required in the future so that more relevant courses can be put in place.

Meritocracy vs welfarism: A middle ground?

One area where the state has historically played a relatively minor role is income redistribution. Taxes and social expenditures are low by international standards, in part to increase the attractiveness of Singapore as a business hub. There are few taxes on wealth or capital gains. Singapore allocates eight percent of its GDP to social spending, comprising mainly education and health expenditures, a much lower portion than that of other developed nations, especially Western European ones (France, for example, spends about 30 percent of its GDP on social spending).[14]

This is a legacy of Lee Kuan Yew's aversion to welfarism. Lee criticized "the folly of populist politicians who win elections playing the politics of equal rewards or egalitarianism: squeeze the successful to pay for the welfare of the poor, and end up with the equalization of poverty."[15] He believed that "high personal taxes dampen the desire of many to achieve wealth and success."[16] There are no unemployment benefits in Singapore and little support is given to retirees who have not saved enough throughout their career. In Lee's view, that role is expected to be filled by the family. He would often compare Confucian societies, where "the individual exists in the context of the family, extended family, friends, and wider society; […] the government cannot and should not take over the role of the family," with western societies, where the government plays a bigger role in "fulfilling the obligations of the family when it fails."[17] Most Singaporeans feel a personal responsibility in taking care of their parents in their old age, just as they expect their children to take care of them when they grow older. The same logic applies to family members in precarious situations.

Apart from education, there are two sectors where the government does provide strong support. One is the healthcare system, considered one of the best by the World Health Organization for its universality, efficiency, and affordability. The other is public housing. Most newly married couples are entitled to purchase an apartment (usually on a 99-year lease basis) at below-market prices. This has resulted in 80 percent of the population living in public housing and 90 percent of Singaporeans owning a property, one of the highest home ownership rates in the world. With property prices surging since 1965, many homeowners have become wealthy, although their wealth may be mostly composed of a rather illiquid asset that most hope to bequest to their children.[18]

Overall though, a combination of low taxes and low social spending has resulted in high income inequalities. Although few statistics are available, wealth inequalities are likely to be high as well in a country where citizens save a large portion of their income and pay few wealth taxes. While all parts of the population have benefited from Singapore's success, there has been growing discontent among some citizens toward rising inequalities and the higher cost of living. Singapore's Gini coefficient is higher compared to most other developed countries after accounting for taxes and transfers and has increased further in the 1990s and early 2000s.[19]

Measures have been taken to remedy the situation. Top tax rates were increased and the annual budget allocated to social benefits almost doubled over the last decade.[20] Low-income earners have fared relatively well in the past decade, better than their peers in most other developed countries. The bottom 20 percent of households with at least one full-time worker have seen their *real* annual income improve in the last 20 years, whereas it has declined in the US.[21] Poorer citizens in Singapore do have better access to housing, healthcare, and education than in many other countries. Social mobility remains relatively high.

But even though low-income earners have on average seen their situation improve, the income of high-earners has grown at a much faster pace. In the three decades that followed independence, inequality was never much of an issue. The economy was booming and people could see that they were doing much better than past generations. But today, improvements in living conditions between the younger generation and the one that preceded it are less obvious. In an age of social media where wealth is more readily displayed, perceptions of unfairness, whether justified or not, exacerbate the discontent of parts of the population.

Should taxes be increased and should more be spent on the economically vulnerable? It is a difficult balance to strike. Reducing taxes and social spending generates higher inequalities. But raising taxes and social benefits too high increases the likelihood that some will evade taxes and abuse benefits, possibly jeopardizing a meritocratic model that has worked so well for the country. Levels of trust in Singapore are "average": higher than in the US or Southern European countries, but lower than Northern European countries. Despite those moderate levels of social trust, Singapore has many safeguards in place to prevent tax evasion and the abuse of social benefits: low levels of corruption, the use of third-party tax reporting, stiff penalties for wrongdoing, and an efficient judiciary. Workers are unlikely to shirk their duties if taxes were to be increased further (but within acceptable limits). Redistributive efforts should therefore be pursued further, though probably not to the extent of what has been done in many European countries.

The risk paradox

A colleague of ours recently told us that his daughter was looking forward to going on a holiday to Europe or the US with a Singaporean friend. The parents of the friend agreed for their daughter to travel to Germany or France, but not to Spain or Italy as those countries were deemed "too dangerous." Anything east of Germany was also not allowed because it was "too close to Ukraine." The US was equally off-limits because the country was considered to be in a "perpetual cycle of mass shootings" and "full of drug addicts." While those places are probably not as safe as Singapore, a tourist taking basic precautions would be perfectly fine.

Singaporeans, by and large, avoid risks. This is not new: Back in 2012, the country's education minister was already concerned by students lacking the drive and confidence to move out of their comfort zone.[22] But with more uncertainty and volatility in the world amid events such as the COVID-19 pandemic, the wars in Ukraine and Gaza, risk aversion in Singapore is likely to have increased in recent years.

A lack of risk-taking is often associated with a lack of entrepreneurship. Indeed, few Singaporeans want to strike out on their own. A 2019 World Economic Forum study found that among those aged 15–35 in Southeast Asia, Singapore has the lowest proportion of youths that aspire to become entrepreneurs.[23] The country boasts a world-class education system, a clear and business-friendly regulatory framework, and general availability of funds to start a business. Those factors should be conducive to more young graduates becoming entrepreneurs. And yet, few will venture down that path. Many young Singaporeans want to be their own bosses, but the few that set up their own businesses will usually invest in overcrowded sectors, such as owning a restaurant or becoming a rideshare driver, which will do little to improve their finances or their nation's competitiveness. Another factor holding back entrepreneurs is a lack of tolerance for failure in Singapore society. An entrepreneur who has failed will tend to be ostracized. In the US, failure at setting up a business is often viewed as a natural progression toward eventual success.

A lack of entrepreneurship is an issue, but perhaps not a critical one. There are few entrepreneurs in South Korea, but that has not prevented the country from becoming highly innovative and having global industry leaders in sectors such as telecommunications, batteries, automobiles, or cosmetics. Innovation and expansion also take place within established companies rather than just start-ups.

Companies in Singapore are very good at improving their internal processes, but perhaps less so at coming up with truly innovative products and services. They also, with very few exceptions, struggle to expand overseas. This is an issue because the domestic market is small and highly competitive, offering few opportunities for further growth. Few Singaporeans are willing to accept overseas postings. A 2021 survey by the American Chamber of Commerce in Singapore highlighted that many Singaporeans are uncomfortable dealing with the uncertainty and ambiguity that come with global rotations.[24] Singapore may have become too successful in providing a very stable and safe environment, reducing the incentive for its citizens to take initiatives and venture outside their comfort zone.

It is rather unusual for such a small country highly dependent on foreign trade to have most of its companies entirely focused on their own domestic market. To be fair, it is more difficult for local companies to expand internationally compared to their peers in many other countries. Companies in the US, China, or Europe (especially since the advent of a common European market) have access to huge markets. A Singapore company looking to expand into Southeast Asia or beyond will have to navigate numerous jurisdictions, languages, currencies, and cultures. But, it can be done. Sweden and Switzerland are examples of countries with a small population that have over the past 50 years established leading companies with a worldwide presence. Young Singaporeans should be encouraged to do some of their studying abroad and accept job offerings overseas to gain a different perspective and a better understanding of the world. This can only benefit their country over time.

China: No longer a distant relative

Singapore has achieved tremendous success since its independence half a century ago not only by putting in place all the right economic policies but also by capitalizing on a hardworking and thrifty population. It has consistently been able to adapt to a changing landscape by anticipating the needs of its economy and actually getting things done. That is unlikely to change.

As a small country with a very limited domestic market, Singapore's economy is much more reliant on global trends compared to larger nations. Any slowdown in global trade will have disproportionate consequences for its economy. The biggest trend affecting Singapore in the past decades has been the rise of China, now its top trading partner. China is also the main recipient of direct investments by Singapore companies.[25] Semiconductors, which represent Singapore's largest manufacturing segment, are mostly sold into China. Chinese banks and tech giants have a significant presence in the island-state. As China moves up the value chain, its manufacturers and service providers are increasingly able to compete on quality and continue to have a cost advantage over Singapore despite rising wages. This represents not only a threat to Singapore but also an opportunity as Chinese consumers increasingly require higher-quality products that Singapore and others are able to supply. By ensuring that its workers acquire the necessary skills to adapt to a changing world, Singapore is well positioned, from a technical, geographical, and cultural perspective to take advantage of this shift in the Chinese market. Four decades after Deng's fateful visit to Singapore and the massive changes it inspired, the destiny of Singapore is increasingly tied to China, for better or worse.

Chapter 3

Sweden

In early 2017, the Swedish tax office voiced a rather unusual complaint: Tax revenues were too *high*. The equivalent of almost US$5 billion in additional taxes was received in 2016 over what had been budgeted. This doubled the budget surplus: Instead of the US$5 billion of expected surplus, the government ended up with a surplus of almost US$10 billion. Most tax offices around the world would be thrilled at the prospect of recovering more tax. Citizens usually try to minimize their tax payments; but in Sweden, taxpayers were intentionally paying too much tax, and authorities were far from impressed.[1]

Swedish taxpayers, already among the most heavily taxed in the world, were not acting out of pure generosity. With short-term interest rates lowered below zero by the Swedish central bank, businesses and individuals were seeing their bank deposits depleted or at best not earning any return. Meanwhile, the tax office was offering a 0.56 percent return for any overpaid taxes. By paying too much tax, Swedish households and businesses were in effect lending money to the government for an interest rate that was higher than if they had kept those funds in their bank account. The tax office had not adjusted interest rates to reflect current market conditions and taxpayers took full advantage. What if the state did not return those funds? And, if it did return the funds, how long would it take? In Sweden, no one had to worry about such matters.

There are few borrowers in the world with better creditworthiness than the Swedish state.

So why was the government unhappy? For several reasons. First, it had to pay a positive return over funds that it could have raised at negative rates. The extra annual cost resulting from the rate differential was estimated at US$90 million.[2] Second, the additional (but temporary) tax revenues created a headache in terms of fiscal budgeting: Overpayments had to be deducted from the 2016 budget to reflect a more accurate picture of revenues and expenditures during that year. Likewise, future budgets had to disregard the extra tax income: US$10 billion of surplus in 2016 would likely not translate into a similar surplus in the following years. Another concern was what to do with the additional tax revenues. Funds could not be used for additional expenses since out-of-budget expenditures required specific approvals; besides, those funds at some stage had to be returned to taxpayers.

The tax office was left with no choice but to ask Swedish taxpayers to pay *less* tax. This somewhat bizarre episode illustrates the relation that Swedes have with their government, one that is based on mutual trust, a value that underpins much of Sweden's economy.

Trust as the foundation of the Nordic model

Together with its Nordic neighbors, Sweden is often described as one of the best-managed economies in the world. Few would disagree with that statement. The country ticks all the right boxes: It maintains one of the highest standards of living and its GDP grows at higher rates compared to most other rich countries. Corruption is almost nonexistent. Its citizens enjoy generous and efficient social services covering education, unemployment, healthcare, childcare, and retirement. Unemployment and inequalities are kept low. No wonder its people are among the happiest in the world.[3]

Countries that have tried to copy the Nordic model of high taxes, high welfare distributions, and low inequalities have rarely achieved similar results. What those countries have failed to realize is that the model is not easily transferable, owing to the high level of trust within Nordic societies. About two-thirds of Swedes generally trust others, a much higher proportion than any of the other 60 countries included in the World Values Surveys.[4] Not only is social trust high but it is also very stable: In the six editions of the World Values Survey since 1981, social trust among Swedes has oscillated between 52 percent and 64 percent. The European Social Survey finds similar results, with all Scandinavian countries scoring much better in social trust than other European nations.[5]

There are many competing theories as to why social trust emerged in Nordic countries and not, say, in Spain or Greece: the sophisticated trade networks and egalitarian Viking societies, the impact of the church when Sweden became Lutheran at the end of the 16th century, the limited influence of aristocracy, the fact that for centuries many peasants owned their estate, or the early development of public institutions. We will never know for sure which factor, or combination of factors, led Swedish citizens to become more trusting of each other. They feel a sense of togetherness, a belief that solutions that benefit one member of society are likely to benefit all of society. The collective is seen as superior to the individual. Companies are organized in flat structures and the advice of more junior team members is often sought. Decision-making is consensual, which delays the process but ensures wide adoption of the decisions made.

Swedes not only trust others but they also trust their political institutions. More than half of them trust their parliament.[6] They see their institutions as stable and efficiently run. This reflects the country's strong political stability: Differences between the two main political parties are relatively minor and ensure political continuity whenever there is a change in government, with both parties generally adopting a pragmatic rather than ideological approach to managing the country that political stability may be at risk with the rise of populist parties for reasons that will be discussed later in this chapter. Public institutions are efficient and transparent. Annual budgets are openly discussed. Any document sent or received by an official can be viewed by the public: Any communication made by a minister to the representative of a public or private company can be made publicly available by request, without the need for that request to be justified. Every professional expense made by politicians, whatever the amount, is publicly available and scrutinized by journalists. In 1995, a minister was accused of using her professional credit card for grocery shopping, purchasing diapers, chocolate bars, and other personal items. She further confessed to having failed to pay on time her parking tickets and bills for her children's day care. The total value of those private expenses was less than US$1,000 and she paid those amounts within a few months. In most countries, such actions would hardly raise an eyebrow, but in Sweden, it created a political storm. The minister was forced to resign.[7] She is not alone: Many politicians have had to step down for flying in business class or residing at hotels considered too luxurious.

High taxes and the distribution of generous benefits have not led to the abuse of public goods. Sweden consistently ranks as one of the least corrupt nations. In a community where people trust each other, they will generally refrain from acquiring wealth or power through illegal means, even if they were likely to get away with it. They would feel embarrassed taking advantage of fellow citizens. In a study that observed how diplomats at the United Nations in New York parked their car on public roads, Swedish diplomats had not recorded a single ticket fine even though, as diplomats, they were not liable to pay for those fines.[8] They respected the law, not because of potential sanctions, but because of the values they grew up with. Trust alone is not sufficient to ensure low corruption. Transparency and the rule of law, which implies an independent judiciary that acts quickly and decisively, are important factors that also contribute to Sweden's very low levels of corruption. There have been a few high-profile corruption scandals involving Swedish politicians and companies over the years, but those cases remain the exception rather than the rule.

Strong trust in others and in political institutions has enabled the Swedish government to play a major role in managing the wealth of its citizens. Swedes not only pay very high taxes (marginal income tax rates can go up to 57 percent) but also receive a lot in return, including free education, affordable, quality healthcare, and comfortable pensions. Those that experience hardship, falling ill or losing their job, can rely on the state to support them. The government essentially manages a large part of the wealth of their citizens on their behalf. It would not be accurate to see this as a net transfer of wealth from the rich to the poor. The welfare system is universal: Everyone gets to benefit from it, irrespective of their level of income or wealth. Swedes expect a large portion of what they give to the state to be returned to them at later stages of their lives or when they experience temporary hardship. While those with a lower income benefit more, the system needs to benefit everyone in order to ensure widespread acceptance. If the system is viewed as fair and legitimate, few high earners will attempt to evade paying their share of taxes (they would anyway struggle to do so in a country where most workers are employees and employers have a duty to share wage data directly with tax authorities). People trust their government to do a good job and trust others to act responsibly.

This has led to a very egalitarian society. Sweden, along with other Nordic countries, has one of the lowest Gini coefficients in the world. Inequalities have gradually increased since the 1980s but remain very low by international comparison. The main reason why Sweden today is less equal than it was in the 1980s is because the model that emerged in the 1970s and 1980s had become untenable.

Pushing the model too far

Once upon a time, a woman called Pomperipossa lived in the land of Monismania and earned a living writing books for children. She loved her country and its people and did not mind paying high taxes every year — until the day she discovered that her taxes came up to 102 percent of her income. That must be a mistake, she thought. But it was true: she really had to pay more taxes than what she earned! Why would she be punished so severely? Was writing books for children something dirty or shameful in any way? She was told that one way to pay less tax was to take a lot of debt and buy a house, but Pomperipossa never liked debt. She had no choice but to stop writing books, for she could not survive without money. She wondered what might happen to independent workers like her or small businesses that similarly struggled with punitive taxes? Would they also perish? And, without all those people and businesses paying their taxes, what might happen to Monismania?

This satirical tale was written in 1976 by children's book author Astrid Lindgren, who was indeed asked to pay 102 percent of income taxes, a result of self-employed workers having to pay both income tax and employer charges.[9] The publication of her tale generated a major debate about tax policy in the country.

In the 1970s and 1980s, the Swedish economy grew very slowly, slower than OECD (a group of rich countries) and European Union nations, culminating in a financial crisis in the early 1990s. Unemployment and public debt increased sharply, inflation stood at 10 percent, and real wages decreased.[10] During those years, Sweden was faced with declining tax revenues and rapidly increasing public expenditures, resulting in a fiscal deficit that reached 10 percent of the GDP. Ever-higher taxes were choking the country's economic activity, creating strong incentives for high-income individuals and businesses to exploit various tax avoidance schemes.[11] In 1990, someone with an income of $100,000 and wealth of $500,000 would have paid about $80,000 in income and wealth taxes, an effective tax rate of 80 percent, leaving that person with just $20,000 in after-tax income. There was a cap to ensure that the accumulation of various taxes did not add up to an "unreasonable" rate. But that cap had been gradually increased and stood at 85 percent of taxable income by the end of the 1980s (in the case of Mrs. Lindgren, the cap was not particularly effective).[12] Those who still managed to accumulate wealth and intended to leave a bequest to their loved ones would have to return almost 70 percent of their assets to the state in the form of inheritance taxes.

It is therefore unsurprising, even in a country where trust in others and in the government is high, that people were becoming increasingly frustrated. Because of the 70 percent inheritance tax, an entrepreneur could not transfer her business from one generation to the other. Instead, she would be forced to sell assets of her company at fire sale prices to cover her tax expenses. For many families, their main asset was their house. When a family member died, the surviving spouse often had to sell the family house to settle their tax bill. The middle class ended up becoming the real victims of the tax system. Top earners would find ways to avoid paying high taxes; numerous loopholes existed, such as setting up a foundation to avoid intergenerational transfer taxes. A more radical option was to emigrate: The most famous examples were Tetra Pak founder Ruben Rausing, IKEA founder Ingvar Kamprad, and industrialist Fredrik Lundberg who all left the country. If low inequalities are the result of high-income earners leaving the country, this is hardly a desirable outcome. The best evidence that those high taxes were not working out as intended is how little they contributed to Swedish finances. At best, inheritance and capital gain taxes contributed 0.4 percent to the annual GDP each. When they were both scrapped in 2004 and 2007, respectively, they were contributing less than 0.2 percent to the annual GDP each.[13] People were evidently finding ways around them.

Starting in the early 1990's, the total tax cap was lowered, individual and corporate tax rates were reduced, an expenditure ceiling was introduced, ministries were made more accountable, the monitoring of public expenses was enhanced, and budgets became more transparent. Those changes greatly improved the legitimacy of Sweden's fiscal system. The flipside is that inequalities increased; they had to because the Gini coefficients achieved in the 1980s were not sustainable as they came at the expense of higher deficits and lower economic growth. The idea was to find the right balance between economic growth and minimal inequalities, a balance that Sweden has, by most accounts, successfully achieved since those reforms.

While inadequate fiscal policies are to be blamed for Sweden's lackluster economic performance of the 1970s and 1980s, the crisis of 1990 also had other origins. Sweden was not the only country in recession: Much of the industrialized world was experiencing a downturn. Swedish banks had become less regulated and made loans to businesses and to the booming real estate market with little consideration for the creditworthiness of borrowers. Another factor was that the central bank was raising rates massively to fend off speculative attacks against the local currency that was pegged to a basket of currencies. When the property bubble burst and businesses started accumulating losses, banks had to be rescued. In the end, a combination of fiscal reforms, currency devaluation, stronger bank regulation, and broad political support for reforms heralded the start of a prolonged period of growth.

Market-driven

In the 1970s and 1980s, many industries were heavily regulated. Shipbuilding and manufacturing of steel, paper and pulp, and textiles were all struggling against lower-cost competitors, mostly from Asia. The government tried to protect its industries by nationalizing and subsidizing them. Tariffs were also imposed on imported goods. Those measures did not reverse the trend: Swedish companies continued to accumulate losses. These were not companies with sound business models and temporary cash flow shortages that needed support to get back on their feet. They were companies that simply could not compete because their production costs were too high. High corporate taxes did little to help. The only employer that was constantly hiring was the state.

Realizing that market forces were required for Swedish companies to regain their competitiveness, the government enacted a series of reforms. With a population of just 10 million, the domestic market offered limited opportunities. Swedes are savers: Gross savings represent 30 percent of GDP, higher than the EU average of 24 percent.[14] With a small domestic market and low domestic consumption, if Swedish firms were to grow, many of them had no choice but to export their goods and services, and if they wanted to export, they needed to be globally competitive.

Government monopolies and regulations that stifled competition were removed. Companies operating in industries in permanent decline were shut down. Trade barriers were lowered, more so in 1995 when Sweden joined the European Union, enacting free trade with other EU members. Sweden's economy is now resolutely turned toward the world: Imports and exports make up a combined 100 percent of the GDP.[15]

The shutdown of non-competitive industries did not result in mass unemployment. The unemployment rate had already reached 10 percent in 1993 and gradually decreased to 5 percent by 2001 (it stood at 8 percent as of December 2023). There was no mass unemployment because inefficient companies made way to new, more competitive ones as Swedish entrepreneurs focused on other industries with better prospects, shifting resources (such as skilled workers and funding) accordingly and creating a host of new businesses where Sweden can really add value. The country has become one of the most innovative nations in the world, regularly featuring at the top of Global Innovation Index rankings. Some of the most well-known examples of successful Swedish start-ups are

Skype, Spotify, and Linux, but there are many others in fields such as biotechnologies and microelectronics. The government plays its part by providing a business-friendly legal framework: Creating new companies is easy and cost-effective, with tax incentives offered to entrepreneurs. The government also provides funding to start-ups through local agencies. Research and development in Sweden represents 3.4 percent of the GDP, higher than the OECD average of 2.8 percent.[16]

Innovation requires an educated workforce. Sweden relies on a strong and affordable educational system. The country's position has however declined in the PISA rankings. The Swedish educational system is now less focused on hard work (less homework, fewer hours at school, and less emphasis on grades), with predictable results. The influx of migrant children, catapulted into a society very different from the one they came from, contributes to the lower national education levels as they, on average, perform more poorly at school.[17]

The automobile sector provides a good example of the process of creative destruction at work. SAAB Automobile and Volvo both ran into major difficulties in 2010. The Swedish government did not intervene to keep either company artificially alive. SAAB Automobile was bankrupted (the company that acquired the bankruptcy estate, NEVS, now produces electric cars for the Chinese market) and Volvo, which had not made a profit since 2005 and was purchased in 2010 by Geely, a Chinese car manufacturer, now sells almost twice as many cars as it did back in 2009 while maintaining most of its workforce in Sweden.[18]

A unique feature of the Nordic model that facilitates a process of creative destruction is the focus on *employability* as opposed to the protection of existing jobs. Unions, which form an integral part of Swedish corporate life, are not ideologically confrontational toward management. They understand that, in a changing world, some jobs will be lost and others created. What is important, not only to them but also to employers, is that displaced workers can transition into new jobs and that they are provided with financial, technical, and psychological support during that transition.

It is ironic that Sweden is often viewed by outsiders as a socialist, centrally planned economy in which the government plays a major role in the destiny of local companies. In fact, the Swedish economy is market-driven, lightly regulated (except for banks), with few trade barriers, and one in which the state only plays a minor role. The total valuation of all publicly owned companies represents less than 10 percent of GDP.[19] Sweden has combined a strong welfare state with markets that are mostly free from governmental intervention. This combination has worked out well for the country, not only by setting up an environment conducive to market forces but also by providing public services and support to individuals whenever they face hardship during their lives. When one is faced with a sudden drop of income, it helps not to have to worry about medical bills or school expenses. A similar point can be made to explain why so many entrepreneurs take the risk of starting a business: If they fail, they know that many of their expenses will be covered.

A model pension system

Support from the state is becoming ever more relevant when it comes to pensions. Sweden's population is aging rapidly, just as it is in most developed countries. The Swedish pension system went through a series of reforms in the 1990s and is quite unique in its current form. Most of the contributions made by employees and employers are recorded on an account and given a rate of return that is linked to the country's real wage growth. When a worker retires, his annual pension payments will be calculated not only based on the value of that account but also based on market conditions and life expectancy, with annual payments adjusted accordingly. This effectively allows the pension system to automatically adjust to cover any shortfall, avoiding the political deadlock that is all too common in other countries that rely on unsustainable pension systems.[20] The main drawback of this system is that retirees, not workers, are the ones suffering the consequences when market conditions deteriorate. This is what happened after the financial crisis when pensions were cut in 2010 and 2011 and the government had to step in with additional funding. But it does make the system more sustainable in the long run.

The sustainability of the Swedish pension system depends to a large extent on the number of people working and contributing. Sweden has the second-highest rate of employment within the European Union at 82 percent; the country believes it needs an employment rate of at least 80 percent to sustain the current welfare system.[21] So far, the proportion of people working has been going up in recent years, due to rapid economic growth, the rise of the gig economy, the rising number of new young migrants, and more hiring by the public sector in part to handle their arrival.[22]

The pension system put in place by Sweden is a model for others to follow. It will probably need to be tweaked along the way as the population grows older to ensure that retirees do not suffer from gradually declining pensions. There is however a more immediate threat, not just to the pension system, but to the overall welfare system.

Trust under threat

The arrival of large numbers of migrants from 2014 to 2017, many of them fleeing armed conflicts, has stoked tensions and reduced social trust in Sweden, threatening its welfare model. A recent study by the Swedish Migration Studies Delegation looked at the impact of migrants on social trust in various municipalities between 2009 and 2017. It was found that social trust had declined in most municipalities, with those municipalities that welcomed more migrants seeing the strongest decline.[23] Sweden welcomed too many migrants and had to backtrack, limiting the number of new arrivals from 2017 and more recently implementing new rules, making it more difficult to obtain permanent residency. Sweden recorded 60 people shot dead in 2022; Norway and Denmark had four each, and Finland only two.[24]

The study made another interesting and more unexpected discovery: Swedes who are in regular contact with those from other backgrounds in the area where they live are more likely to trust others. In other words, by interacting regularly with migrants, people tend to trust them more. Of course, that is not always the case and depends on the openness and the behavior of both locals and migrants. But more human interaction usually results in a better understanding and appreciation for the other person. In many countries, those living in large cities will have more interactions with migrants and will often have a more positive opinion of them.

Similar to previous waves of migration, the latest one should ultimately benefit an aging Swedish society, as long as migrants are able to adapt to their new environment. That means learning the local language, understanding how local institutions work, and integrating with locals. This is easier said than done. Most migrants lack the necessary qualifications to find a job. But it is the only way for them to contribute to their new society and be accepted as an integral part of it.

Northern lights

Declining social trust threatens the Nordic welfare model, a model unique to the region that has enabled it to maintain relatively equal societies at a time when much of the world suffers from widening inequalities. After the Swedish economy went into a free fall as the system was pushed too far, a series of reforms in the 1990s rescued the banks, removed the excesses of the welfare state without jeopardizing its role as the main provider of financial security, introduced much-needed market reforms, and put in place effective, transparent, and accountable institutions. Those reforms were the start of a period of strong and continuous prosperity.

The citizens of Sweden may be a bit less trusting of others than they used to be, in part as a result of the recent mass migration onto their shores, but they remain some of the most trusting people on the planet. High levels of trust also helped the country during the COVID-19 pandemic. The controversial decision to not enforce lockdowns and other restrictions at the height of the COVID-19 outbreak resulted in more cases and deaths compared to other Nordic countries (adjusted for population size), but the numbers remained much lower compared to most other European nations that went into lockdowns, largely as a result of Swedes trusting their government and following its recommendations.

As long as it is able to maintain high levels of trust, Sweden's economy should continue to do very well. Its entrepreneurial and environmentally conscious population is well positioned to transition to a more digital and green economy. This is also the case for other Nordic countries. Those nations already enjoy some of the highest standards of living anywhere in the world. Because values cannot simply be transposed and imposed to others, the Nordic model cannot be replicated elsewhere, at least not in its entirety. But there is much to learn from it.

Chapter 4

Botswana

In 1954, geologists working in the scorching heat of the Kalahari Desert, located in what was known at the time as the British Protectorate of Bechuanaland, took interest in unlikely creatures: termites. As they observed the mounds created by those insects, they discovered that some of them contained tiny fragments of a black mineral. They were puzzled by how those fragments ended up in those mounds. More importantly, they wanted to know what the mineral was.

For mounds to be constructed, termites require wet mud. They will dig until they can find the water bed, which in the case of the Kalahari Desert typically sits at 100 feet or further below the ground. As they returned to the surface, they would at times carry with them tiny traces of various rocks. Geologists analyzed those traces and found that some of them contained kimberlite, a rare type of rock which got its name from the town of Kimberley in South Africa that became famous in the nineteenth century for its discovery of diamonds. It would take another decade and more advanced technology for actual kimberlite to be found. Botswana opened its first diamond mine in 1967 and began extracting and exporting the precious stones a few years later. Today, it is the largest diamond producer in the world.

At around the same time that geologists began prospecting for diamonds in the Kalahari Desert, a 33-year-old man by the name of Seretse

Khama was living in exile in England, banned for life from returning to his native Bechuanaland for having married a white woman while studying in London, an act that the British could not tolerate in a region torn by racial conflicts. Khama's father was the ruler of one of the main tribes in Bechuanaland and his son had been destined to succeed him. The British set up a judicial enquiry to prove that Khama was unfit to lead his chieftaincy. When the resulting report concluded the opposite, that Khama was eminently fit to rule, the report was suppressed by the British government for 30 years. The couple was eventually allowed to return to Bechuanaland in 1956 under the condition that they remained ordinary citizens. Khama tried his hand at raising cattle, with limited success. He did however climb the political ranks quickly and became Botswana's first president when the country gained its independence in 1966. He inherited a country that was among the poorest in Africa, let alone in the world.

At that stage, many things could have gone wrong. Too many African countries have descended into civil war and widespread corruption, especially those "blessed" with valuable natural resources. But Botswana defied the odds. Over the next 30 years, the small landlocked country experienced the highest economic growth rate per capita *in the world*. Its GDP per capita today rivals that of Mexico or Turkey. Every year, the country tops the list of least-corrupted African nations and has become an economic model for the continent and beyond.

Diamond windfall

The discovery and extraction of diamonds has had an enormously positive impact on Botswana's economy. Economists sometimes downplay the role of diamonds, instead focusing on other factors such as the leadership of Khama and his successors, the rise of institutions, the fact that British colonial forces never became heavily involved in the running of the country prior to independence, and the consultation and consensus-seeking behavior that is prevalent in Tswana culture, by far the main ethnic group of Botswana. It is likely that each of these factors played a role in Botswana's growth. But without diamonds, Botswana would never have reached its current state of development. Saudi Arabia, another nation heavily reliant on natural resources (oil and gas account for half of its national income), has a GDP per capita three times higher than Botswana. Yet, Saudi Arabia is hardly recognized for the quality of its institutions or the leadership of its rulers. Strong leadership and governance in other African countries devoid of natural resources have also led to growth, but nowhere close to what Botswana has achieved.

Although numbers vary from year to year, reflecting the cyclical nature of the industry, diamonds typically account for more than 70 percent of Botswana's exports and at least a third of all GDP. Reliance on diamonds was in fact even greater in the 1980s, when it accounted for half of the country's GDP.[1] This only comprises the *direct* contribution made by diamonds to the local economy; many other industries indirectly rely to some extent on diamonds. Because of diamond revenues, Botswana earns at least a third of additional income every year that it can spend on improving its the livelihood of its people. To put this into perspective, it is as if the US, with an annual GDP of US$23 trillion, earned an extra US$7 trillion each year from its natural resources (the actual contribution of natural resources to its GDP is less than 1 percent). This would comfortably allow the US to finance its entire federal deficit. Botswana's economy could never have prospered as much as it did without diamonds. This sizable additional source of revenue makes it that much easier to run a budget and pay public servants well, provide free education, and build foreign currency reserves. The clearest evidence of the economy's dependency on diamonds is that when global demand for diamonds drops, the country quickly falls into recession.

Fighting corruption: A rare African success

Diamonds, however, are no guarantee of economic success. Sierra Leone, another large diamond producer, has a coastline, is closer to destination markets in Europe or the US, and benefits from much more rainfall than Botswana. If one had to place a bet in 1970 as to which of the two countries would fare better, Sierra Leone was the obvious candidate. Yet today, Sierra Leone remains one of the poorest countries in the world, mired in civil conflicts during most of its modern history. Too many African nations have been cursed in some form or another by their natural resources.

This is where the actions taken by Seretse Khama and his successors have been crucial. The first step was to recognize that the country lacked the required knowledge to capitalize on its huge reserves of diamonds and would instead have to rely on foreign expertise. Debswana was set up as a partnership with De Beers, the largest diamond company in the world, to discover, extract, and commercialize diamonds. The government agreed to share the profits derived from diamonds with De Beers in exchange for their technical and commercial expertise and did not attempt to arbitrarily renegotiate that agreement every time diamond prices went up, a common trend in many resource-rich African nations. De Beers for its part did not attempt to plunder the country's resources for a short-term gain. To this day, Debswana represents a rare example of a successful partnership between a sub-Saharan government and a foreign company.

Too often, African governments use their natural resources to extract bribes, enriching a few individuals at the expense of the wider population. Seretse Khama had the same deep aversion for corruption as Singapore's Lee Kuan Yew and put in place anti-corruption measures (strong punishments to offenders, transparency in granting government contracts, and open debates on budgets) that are not very different from those in Singapore. Although Khama's successors continued his anti-corruption crusade, they were perhaps less uncompromising.

A series of graft scandals in the 1980s and 1990s, from public land sold to politicians for a pittance to loans granted by local banks to ministers at highly favorable conditions, led to the creation in 1994 of Botswana's anti-corruption agency, the Directorate on Corruption and Economic Crime (DCEC). While an important step in the right direction, the DCEC is not fully independent from the president, who has the right to appoint its director and prevent access to certain documents on the basis of "national security." The corollary to this structure is that if the president is not committed to fighting corruption, the DCEC is unlikely to perform its tasks effectively. Government officials are sometimes accused of nepotism, earning their position through family members and other connections. Some also hold senior executive positions in private companies, blurring the line between public and private offices and increasing the potential for conflicts of interest.

Despite those shortcomings, Botswana has consistently ranked as the least corrupt country in Africa. It was ranked 35th in the world by Transparency International in 2022, scoring better than Poland and Italy.[2] This is a remarkable achievement given the widespread corruption in Africa and the very low social trust that exists in Botswana, with only 10–15 percent of the population believing that people can generally be trusted.[3] The judiciary in Botswana, inherited from the English criminal legal system, is genuinely independent from the government, with private property rights strictly enforced. The Constitution expressly forbids the nationalization of private assets. Successive presidents have reaffirmed their stance against corruption and generally acted accordingly, despite some of the shortcomings described earlier. Botswana's public sector has been mostly meritocratic when it comes to recruitment, compensation, and promotions. Public servants are relatively well paid, which reduces their incentive to accept money or favors, and are warned about the severe penalties in accepting bribes even for the smallest of amounts. Citizens are able to report cases of corruption without fear of retaliation, and swift action is usually taken against those found guilty of such acts.

Spending wisely

The government has historically played a large and positive role in managing the economy. Upon independence, with very few private companies in operation, the state had no choice but to take matters in its own hands. A few years later, it would also manage the increasing revenues derived from the extraction and sale of diamonds. But instead of diverting diamond revenues for corrupt or frivolous purposes, diamond proceeds were spent on improving social and economic conditions, in particular infrastructure, education, and healthcare. From the 1970s onward, the pace of construction accelerated, with new roads, commercial offices, schools, universities, and hospitals built. Such investments require large savings. The country saves about 40 percent of its income, a much higher figure compared to other African nations. The government has been able to run surpluses during most years, enjoying large revenues from diamonds while adopting a conservative approach to public expenditures. Khama's frugality was legendary, a reflection of the thrifty nature of the Botswanan people. Conferences would be held at local hotels to avoid the cost of building large facilities, ministers were barred from flying first class (in an era when the only other alternative was economy class), and public officials on international duty had to make their calls at the crack of dawn when long-distance calls were cheaper.[4] This cautious approach to spending ensured that diamond revenues would not be squandered. Government budgets are devised every 6 years, ensuring continuity and reducing the temptation for the government to go on a spending spree whenever diamond revenues increase.

Significant investments were also made in education. As a highly educated person himself, Khama understood the importance of an educated workforce to take his country to higher levels of development and ensure that local firms were able to learn from and compete with foreign companies. Schools were built in both urban and rural areas. Foreign teachers were not asked to leave, as was often the case in countries gaining independence; they were instead asked to remain so that they could transmit their knowledge to the local population. To this day, Botswana continues to invest heavily in education, up to 9 percent of the GDP and 20 percent of the country's national budget, high figures by international comparison.[5]

Primary education is free, with most children attending and completing it. Two-thirds of students who complete primary school enroll for secondary school, which is not compulsory. Dropout rates at secondary schools are similarly low at just 1 percent.[6] Courses are taught in the two official languages of the country, Setswana and English. Although Setswana is much more commonly used, students who are able to converse, read, and write in English gain a valuable skill in a country that relies heavily on mineral exports and increasingly on tourism. This has resulted in high literacy rates: 90 percent for the overall population and up to 98 percent for Botswanans aged 18–24 are literate.[7] Botswana fares better compared to the surrounding countries of Mozambique, Namibia, and South Africa in both reading and numerical literacy.[8]

Despite the progress made, many challenges remain. Although heavy investments continue to be made in the education system and most of the population is highly literate, many students who complete secondary school are not equipped with the necessary skills to enter the workforce. The quality of education remains low: Students in Botswana may do better than their immediate neighbors, but they lag behind in international comparisons, in mathematics and science.[9] High levels of unemployment reflect the fact that the diamond industry is not very labor-intensive, and also that local companies struggle to find qualified workers.

Despite all the money spent by the government, the quality of education in Botswana is constrained by 2 factors: hard work (more on this later) and teachers. Although teachers are relatively well paid, they are for the most part not well trained, especially in rural areas. Many aspiring teachers do complete a college degree that specializes in education, but only receive six weeks of practical training. Their performance in the classroom is rarely monitored. In a society with little social trust, teachers who are well paid and have a secure job may not put in the effort required. A 2012 study found that, on average, primary school teachers complete only 60 percent of the curriculum.[10] The authors of the study emphasize the very slow pace in conducting classes, which is partially attributed to the fact that some teachers struggle with the technicality of the curriculum. Teacher absenteeism is not an issue though, with absenteeism rates much lower than those of neighboring countries.[11]

Such shortcomings should not overshadow the tremendous progress that Botswana's education system has made since independence. But to progress further, there needs to be more emphasis on better training of teachers, with their performance regularly assessed and remedies applied if their performance falls below expectations. Comparatively high wages and the difficulty in finding jobs in Botswana should allow the country to be more selective when recruiting and maintaining teachers in their positions, at least in larger cities.

Open for business

In the years that followed independence, the role of the government was gradually curtailed as many public companies were privatized. In the late 1960s and 1970s, at a time when the governments of developing countries were pondering the merits of communism, Seretse Khama favored a market-oriented approach, one in which companies could operate freely. Registering a new company is a fairly straightforward process, and so is the winding down of uncompetitive firms. Few restrictions apply to trade within the country. Telecommunications, energy, and aviation have been earmarked for privatization in the coming years (the telecoms sector was partially privatized in 2016). Botswana's early leaders shared Deng Xiaoping and Lee Kuan Yew's disdain for ideological considerations, focusing instead on practical results. As Quett Masire, the man who succeeded Khama as president, put it, "If it works, we do it, and we don't care what it's called."[12]

With valuable resources to sell and a very limited domestic market (the population is only 2.6 million), Botswana's policymakers understood that strong growth would only be possible by opening the country's borders, focusing on exports. Apart from diamonds, another historically important sector is cattle. In 1975, Botswana negotiated a free trade agreement with Europe for the export of beef and veal. Seretse Khama was also actively involved in the revamping of the Southern African Customs Union in 1969, a free trade agreement between countries in the region, including South Africa.

Foreign companies have historically been welcomed into Botswana and are not discriminated against. There are no foreign exchange controls, a rarity in Africa. Foreign companies can fully own their local subsidiaries and are therefore not required to enter into partnerships with local entities. No restriction applies on the repatriation of profits, capital gains, or debt servicing.

Companies investing in Botswana are also comforted by the fact that the country has been an island of political stability since independence, generally free of conflicts in a continent known for its instability. Despite holding elections every 5 years, the same party has been in power throughout, ensuring continuity and long-term decision-making. Even in the early 1980s when Botswana struggled with lower revenues from diamonds and was forced to implement austerity measures, the ruling party was never seriously challenged. The government derives its legitimacy not only from the economic prosperity generated but also because of its highly homogeneous population, with more than 80 percent belonging to the

Tswana ethnic group. When he took over the reins of his country, Khama suppressed the authority of local tribal chiefs so that power would reside with the central government. Local tribal chiefs are included in the political process but act mostly on a consultative basis, without real legislative power. Khama achieved this by sharing revenues from diamonds with all parts of the country, being careful not to favor his own tribe, even though diamond mines were mostly located within his tribe's territory.

Not quite cutting-edge

For all its achievements, Botswana remains stuck as a middle-income nation. The spectacular growth it achieved during the first three decades of its modern existence has not carried on in the twenty-first century. The official unemployment rate has stood stubbornly above 20 percent for the working-age population and above 30 percent for those below 25 years of age; the real figures are probably higher. The diamond sector provides few job opportunities, accounting for less than three percent of all jobs in the country.[13] Starting in 2011, the authorities pushed for more value to be created within the country: Instead of just extracting and exporting raw diamonds, Botswana reached an agreement with De Beers to establish a sorting plant in the capital city of Gaborone and have more cutting and polishing done locally. Botswana's main competition in diamond cutting and polishing is India, with about 600,000 workers in that industry, predominantly in the state of Maharashtra.[14] If a fraction of those jobs moved to Botswana, the country's unemployment rate would drop significantly.

It has not quite worked out that way. Although wages in Botswana are similar to those in India, Indian cutters are able to cut and polish two to three times as many diamonds as their Botswanan counterparts.

De Beers estimates the costs of cutting and polishing a carat of diamond to be $60–$120 in Botswana but only $10–$50 in India. Botswanan workers are just not productive enough.[15] Companies often prefer to hire foreign workers from neighboring countries such as Zimbabwe who tend to display a more diligent attitude toward work. The various efforts by successive governments since the 1980s to improve labor productivity have so far yielded few results.

Inequalities: A quick fix?

The country may have grown spectacularly, but it has also become one the most unequal societies in the world, the third most unequal according to the World Bank. It is common for countries experiencing rapid growth to have widening inequalities: some people will inevitably become richer faster than others. But in Botswana, inequalities are exacerbated by the sharp contrast between well-educated city dwellers and a poorly educated rural population mostly employed in agriculture. Agriculture represents less than 3 percent of the GDP but employs more than a quarter of the working population.[16]

Things have improved over the past decade. By providing subsidies, loans, and government jobs to the most vulnerable, inequalities and extreme poverty have been reduced, though they remain high. Yet handing cash and unproductive jobs to the poor is hardly a long-term solution. As revenues from diamonds dwindle, securing enough funding to subsidize the poor will increasingly become a challenge. Most of the jobs created have come from the government, contributing to a more bloated sector that now accounts for half of total employment.[17] A large public sector is not necessarily a bad thing, as long as it remains meritocratic, efficient, and innovative. Yet a growing number of citizens are becoming overly dependent on the state, negatively affecting productivity and growth.

A ceiling to growth

What Botswana has accomplished since independence is exceptional. Countries around the world and in Africa in particular should study Botswana and seek to emulate its achievements. The Southern African nation has ticked almost all the right boxes in managing its rich mineral resources and putting in place the right policies. Botswanan citizens have enjoyed much higher standards of living since independence, with better education and low corruption.

Over the years, the government has launched many initiatives in a bid to further improve the living conditions of its people. It has provided funding to projects in manufacturing, tourism, and agriculture, supports small and medium enterprises, aims to make Botswana an innovation and logistics hub in the region, experimented with free trade zones, and diversified into textiles, leather, automotive parts, or financial services to reduce its dependence on diamonds and industrialize the nation further.[18]

And yet, despite the best intentions of Botswana's leaders, little has come out of those initiatives. The country has not managed to specialize and become a market leader in any industry. Too many are still working in the agriculture sector and productivity remains low. Because of a low work ethic, creating a ceiling to higher growth, Botswana will most likely never join the ranks of developed nations, even with the best policies in place.

Not only will higher growth be difficult to achieve but maintaining current growth rates is also becoming a challenge. Continued reliance on diamonds is likely to cause strong headwinds to the economy in the future. As it turns out, diamonds are not forever: Younger people around the world are not buying as much jewelry as their parents or grandparents did. Synthetic diamonds are also becoming more popular. While global demand for diamonds is declining, Botswana's own supply is being depleted: The country is expected to run out of diamonds within a few decades. COVID-19 also negatively affected the industry, with Debswana's sales falling by 30 percent in 2020, although revenues have since rebounded with the reopening of borders and businesses as well as the fall of exports from Russia.[19] In October 2023, after years of negotiations, the agreement with De Beers was amended to allow Botswana to sell a larger portion of its diamond production. De Beers will also invest up to US$75 million in the diversification of the local economy.[20]

One area of diversification holding promise is tourism. Diamonds are not Botswana's only natural resources: Its scenery and wildlife make it an attractive tourism destination. Tourism has grown in the past few years to represent more than 10 percent of GDP. But tourism alone will not compensate for declining diamond revenues. Whatever the future holds for Botswana, its people can be proud of the progress made out of very humble beginnings. Above all, they were blessed with an exceptional leader. Seretse Khama may not be a well-known figure outside of Southern Africa, but he is a giant of history in his own right, championing multi-racial reforms and transforming the economic destiny of his nation.

Chapter 5

India

A typical garment producer in India in the 1980s was a struggling one. Small, family-owned businesses generated barely enough revenues to make a living. Frequent power shortages meant that machines remained idle for extended periods of time. Workers could not be retrenched, even if sales plummeted. As a result, few businesses were hiring when volumes increased. Not that those volumes could rise by much: Producers were not allowed to grow beyond a certain size. There was little incentive to try to make money: Those few producers that accumulated profits would see their electricity and tax bills increase disproportionately as the subsidies they enjoyed were redirected to more needy competitors. Struggling businesses were often rescued by the state. Without any ability to grow and become profitable, no business bothered to invest in equipment and machinery, most of which were decades old. Authorities routinely, and often arbitrarily, set the price at which garments could be sold, at times below the cost of production. Even customers could not always be freely chosen, with businesses forced to sell some of their production to specific companies or individuals. Cotton transported from one state to another required official and unofficial duties to be paid. Trucks would be stuck for hours, if not days, at state borders. Producers focused on low-quality apparel because that was all they could sell in the country. There certainly was demand for higher-quality clothing in richer countries, but those markets were out of reach as India isolated itself from the rest of the world. Corruption pervaded every stage of the supply chain. Most businesses were unregistered and foreign goods were smuggled into the country.[1]

Things have improved dramatically since those dark days, yet many problems persist. Power shortages are less common but still occur. Most producers remain small, inefficient businesses. And corruption is still very much present. Those factors explain why, if you live outside of India, you would likely not have come across a piece of clothing that came with a "Made in India" tag. China, Vietnam, Sri Lanka, and Bangladesh are much more common origins. Bangladesh produces more apparel than India despite a population eight times smaller. The Indian textile industry only represents a small portion of the country's economy even though India is one of the largest cotton producers and benefits from cheap and plentiful labor.

The issues that plague the Indian textile industry and the wider manufacturing sector are almost entirely policy-driven. Despite significant improvements over the last three decades, manufacturing in India remains far less competitive compared to China and other nearby countries. Services, on the other hand, are much less regulated and have been the main driver of India's economic rise.

India becoming

The changes that have swept through India in the past three decades cannot be overstated. After the country embarked on much needed reforms in the early 1990s, reducing trade barriers, allowing foreign investments, and ending many state monopolies, a new nation emerged and with it an ambitious and entrepreneurial generation that no longer aimed to secure government jobs but aspired to become rich. Those reforms ushered in an era of prosperity that propelled the nation of more than a billion people into one of the largest economies in the world. The number of people below the poverty line (defined as those earning less than a dollar per day) has been halved, child mortality has been reduced by two-thirds, the spread of diseases has been halted, and drinking water is now available to most residents, including in rural areas.[2]

Akash Kapur, a writer who relocated back to India after spending most of his life in the United States, describes in his book *India Becoming* how the country he knew as a boy had transformed itself: farmland giving way to high-rise office buildings, global cities that became capitals of finance and technology, a surge in economic activity that improved the livelihoods of millions; but also, a more consumerist and materialistic society and the struggle of some, often belonging to older generations or living in the countryside, in adapting to this new reality.[3] A striking feature about his book is that he could just as well be describing China, which went through a very similar process when it enacted its own sweeping reforms at around the same time.

India is one of the most diverse countries in the world, encompassing many languages, religions, castes, and tribes. Each state wields considerable political and economic power; federal policies can be implemented in different ways across states. Workers in the western state of Gujarat earn, on average, three times as much as those in the impoverished northern state of Bihar.[4] Some communities fare better than others: the Jain community represents less than 1 percent of India's population, but consistently ranks as the wealthiest and most literate of the country.[5] Yet despite their diversity, Indians share similar values and are overwhelmingly committed to national unity. And although aggregate figures may hide strong disparities between the country's regions, national economic trends can certainly be identified.

One such trend is the emergence of a large private sector following the 1990s reforms. More competitive and more efficient than their public counterparts, private firms quickly grew their market share. They have performed best in the services sector, which has grown from 43 percent of the GDP in 1990 to 53 percent of the GDP in 2022.[6] In financial services, private banks now make up 30 percent of all banking activity and are much more profitable than state-owned ones that routinely struggle with bad debts and mismanagement. In aviation, Air India, which has not made a profit since 2007, is left with a market share of just 13 percent, unable to compete with the likes of the privately owned Indigo (this may well change following the sale in January 2022 of the airline to the privately owned Tata Group, the original founder of the airline). 45 percent of schoolchildren now attend private schools, while 60 percent of hospitals beds are privately owned.[7] The information technology (IT) sector is often viewed by those outside of India as providing back-office functions to international businesses, which was indeed the case in the 1990s and early 2000s. Today, that sector has moved up the value chain and offers programming, financial analysis, consulting, and many other services to local and global companies, accounting for 10 percent of GDP.[8]

The services sector could prosper because the state imposed few regulations and trade barriers were mostly removed. Foreign companies were welcomed into the country, especially in IT and banking, employing millions of workers. In fact, the state played a positive role in that process by setting up institutes of technology back in the 1950s which created a small but highly educated intellectual elite that could compete with international companies and learn from them. Weak domestic demand for IT services in the 1990s meant that Indian companies had no choice but to export their services in order to grow. Contrary to manufacturing, services providers were not restricted in the number of people they could employ. Many of them grew to a size that allowed them to compete internationally.

Man-eating lions

The enduring success of the services sector and the wider economy would not have been possible without a hardworking population. One only needs to observe Indian migrants toiling at construction yards across the Middle East, busy executives climbing up corporate ladders, or students diligently preparing for their exams to realize that hard work is ingrained in most Indians as a gateway to a better life. And a better life is increasingly about getting rich. Perhaps this materialism stems from religious beliefs: Wealth accumulation in Hinduism, by far the largest religion practiced in India, is seen in a positive light because it allows people to fulfill their duties to their families and to society.[9] Perhaps it is the extreme competition among 1.4 billion citizens that forces people to work harder in order to secure the best available jobs. India's youth (the country's median age is only 27) is often described as highly ambitious and entrepreneurial.[10] A survey by a consultancy showed that 70 percent of Indian workers would continue to work 5 days a week, even when given the opportunity to work for fewer days for the same salary.[11]

Indians working abroad fall into two categories. The highly educated, highly skilled ones who, on average, become highly successful wherever they relocate. Indians in most developed countries attract the highest wages, in part because they represent the most highly skilled and most highly educated portion of their population. In the UK, Indians earn more than White British and Indian pupils perform better at school than White British pupils.[12] In the US, Indian Americans have the highest income levels of any ethnic group, including White Americans.[13] The other category comprises those with little education and fewer skills, willing to work hard for a low income, mainly in the Middle East or Southeast Asia. Those workers are usually not given permanent residency and return to India after a few years. As such, there are few examples of low-skilled Indians permanently relocating to other countries. But there is at least one, in which Indians started at the very bottom of society and became highly successful within a generation or two.

In 1896, after much deliberation, the British Parliament authorized the construction of a railway linking the interior of Uganda to the port of Mombasa in Kenya, both British colonies at the time, for what became known as the Uganda Railway. Britain was keen to open the interior of Kenya and link it to Uganda to counter the German influence in the region, who were present in what now constitutes Tanzania, Rwanda, and Burundi. A railway would also make Uganda's raw materials such as cotton more accessible.

Building a railway line requires a lot of manpower, even more so back in those days. Deeming the local workforce not up to the task, the British looked toward its largest colony: India. 32,000 Indians were recruited, mostly Sikhs from Punjab, Gujaratis, and Sindhis. Some had been trained as engineers, having worked on the construction of railway lines in India half a century earlier, but most of them were unskilled laborers. Working conditions were brutal. Workers had to contend with long hours, oppressive heat, hostile tribes, inhospitable jungles, diseases such as malaria and black fever, and even man-eating lions. The Tsavo man-eaters (named after the Kenyan region that they came from) were a pair of lions that killed anywhere between 28 and 100 workers during the construction of the railway. Because of the dangers and the exorbitant costs involved, the railway became known as the "lunatic line." 2,500 workers perished. With a railway length of 660 miles, it equates to four workers who lost their lives for every mile.

When the railway opened in 1901, some workers went back to India, but many stayed on. Some continued to work for the railways, others took jobs as artisans, traders, clerks, or administrators. They were soon joined by other migrants from India. Many were the target of persecution, expropriation and discrimination, first by their colonial masters and then by the local population, suspicious of their achievements. They were even forced out of their own country, Uganda, when in 1972 its ruthless dictator Idi Amin Dada gave Ugandans of foreign origin, mostly Ugandan Indians, 90 days to leave the country, threatening them with death if they did not comply. India was not overly enthusiastic to take them back; many ended up in the UK, becoming "twice migrants" and forming an important part of Britain's Indian diaspora.

Despite all the hardship they faced, most Indians in East Africa prospered, evolving into a flourishing professional community. Indians constitute about one percent of the population of Kenya, Mozambique, Uganda, and Tanzania, but they dominate the economies of those countries and feature prominently in local lists of the wealthiest citizens.[14] It is through their hard work, a value transmitted from one generation of Indians to the next, that they have, on average, done very well for themselves.

Manufacturing and agriculture: Overregulated, under-governed

India's success in services has not been replicated in agriculture or manufacturing, sectors in which the state has been much more involved. Market forces have remained shackled because of excessive regulation, preventing businesses from operating on a level playing field. A small number of large manufacturing companies, such as Reliance Industries or Arcelor Mittal, have a global presence and are market leaders in their respective sectors. But too many manufacturers are struggling with low productivity, unable to compete with larger domestic and global players.

The most glaring obstacle to growth in manufacturing was a law (now mostly repealed) that restricted the capital stock of several industries, effectively preventing businesses from growing beyond a certain size. Stringent manufacturing labor laws represent another restriction to higher growth. In some states, firms with more than 100 employees require governmental approval to retrench workers, an approval rarely granted. Such restrictions have led to two consequences. First, most manufacturers are very small: More than 85 percent of them employ fewer than 10 employees (in China, only 5 percent of manufacturing firms have fewer than 10 employees). In the apparel sector, more than 85 percent of Indian companies employ fewer than 8 workers.[15] That prevents companies from benefiting from economies of scale and becoming competitive in international markets. Second, by preventing firms from dismissing workers, companies struggle with overcapacity during economic downturns and are more hesitant to hire new staff during periods of higher growth. The inability to retrench workers has also meant that manufacturers are racing to automate their processes despite the availability of cheap, but not necessarily skilled, labor.[16] Unsurprisingly, states with more flexible labor laws have been found to grow faster and be more productive than those with stricter labor laws.[17]

As China developed its manufacturing capacity on its coastline to be closer to global markets, Indian producers were often forced to build their plants inland because the largest tax concessions were offered in remote areas in an attempt to develop those regions. This created uncompetitive production units and meant that factories would be relocated as soon as tax policies were amended.[18] Add to that a weak infrastructure and restrictions in transporting goods from one state to another and it is clear why most manufacturers in India have struggled.

As for agriculture, it now represents less than a fifth of India's GDP, but still employs more than half of the labor force.[19] This is the most heavily regulated sector and, unsurprisingly, the least efficient. The price of several agricultural products (including wheat, rice, and cotton) is set below market prices to ensure that those products remain affordable to the poorest sections of the population. But price controls that favor consumers often go against the interests of farmers, who require subsidies to survive. Most farms operate on a very small scale. Even if they could invest in higher technology, most do not have the critical size to make those investments worthwhile. This lack of productivity means that the country ends up importing products such as cereals or fertilizers even though it is a producer of both. As will be discussed in another chapter, China has achieved much higher standards of living among its agricultural population through the adoption of better technology and less regulation.[20]

A large public sector has also prevented India's manufacturing sector from growing to its potential. One-third of state-owned enterprises lose money; the ones that do make money often enjoy monopolies and generate margins that are a fraction of those of private competitors.[21] Too often, they are headed by managers who are underpaid given their responsibilities, increasing the incentive to engage in corrupt acts. State-owned banks, whose publicly traded stocks trade at a significant discount to private lenders, accumulate loans that rarely get repaid and require regular recapitalizing by the state. In the electricity sector, most companies are state-owned and virtually all electricity distributors are bankrupt because a quarter of all the electricity they sell is never paid for. It is not paid for because it is stolen, because no meter has been put in place to measure the electricity consumed, or simply because consumers do not pay and distributors do not bother trying to recover the amounts due.[22] State workers have little incentive to perform to their best because their job is guaranteed and their wages are not linked to their performance. Teachers may not bother showing up for class and judges are under no pressure to expedite court cases. The result is inefficient public companies, poor education, and slow justice. One solution is privatization, preferably in an orderly and gradual manner, but that often means laying off workers from state companies, something that no politician wants to be responsible for, even if it generates higher growth and better employment conditions in the longer run.

Sab chor hain[a]

The overreaching arm of the state in the economy has led to higher corruption. In 2005, authorities investigating a potential fraud in the northern state of Uttar Pradesh discovered that trucks used to transport subsidized food grains to the poor had gone missing. Food grains and

---

[a] "Everyone's a thief" in Hindi.

fuel are distributed in every state at highly subsidized prices to those below the poverty line, typically by rail and then by truck. Investigators also found that the registration numbers provided for some trucks in fact belonged to scooters. Transporting 18 tons of food grain (the typical capacity of a truck) on the back of a scooter over hundreds of miles seemed rather unlikely. Food grains and fuel were being diverted from the poor and sold at market prices, with intermediaries pocketing the difference. Some of the food was eventually exported to Bangladesh, Nepal, and even South Africa. It is believed that as much as US$30 billion worth of food and fuel were diverted in a scam that lasted almost 10 years. Thousands of people are alleged to have taken part. If everyone had been convicted and jailed, new prisons would have been required to house all the prisoners.[23]

This is not an isolated case. It is estimated that less than half of all subsidized food grains actually reach the poor.[24] Nor is it the only large fraud case uncovered in Uttar Pradesh: Between 2007 and 2012, US$1.3 billion of public funds that were earmarked for healthcare improvements in rural areas, such as the purchase of medicine, surgical equipment, and hospital upgrades, were found to have been embezzled.[25] Misappropriation of public funds too often makes the news headlines. In 2014, a legislator went as far as proposing a new bill called the Right to Bribe that would legalize bribery (the bill did not proceed).[26]

Heavy price distortions and a lack of transparency are a recipe for corrupt practices because people have a higher incentive to take advantage of the price discrepancy and a higher probability of getting away with it. Most land titles are unclear because land purchases are not properly registered. A vast majority of land titles are subject to dispute, creating a fertile ground for corrupt practices. The country ranks 85th in the Transparency International rankings. There is little accountability in a country where, in the words of Infosys founder Narayana Murthy, "the more important you are, the less answerable you are."[27]

We are not arguing for the abolition of all subsidies, especially in agriculture, which could potentially lead to famine following episodes of drought. The country's public distribution system was praised during droughts in the states of Maharashtra and West Bengal in the 1970s as the food supplies was delivered to those most affected. But the more prices are distorted, the higher the risk that the system gets abused and that beneficiaries remain dependent on state aid. Price controls should be kept at a minimum and only deployed in case of real need by the most vulnerable parts of the population.

High social trust reduces the incentive for corrupt practices, whereas a lack of social trust encourages it. Prime Minister Narendra Modi lamented the lack of trust among Indian citizens as the "biggest issue; the atmosphere of trust can change a lot of things."[28] According to the World Values Survey, only 17 percent of Indians felt that people could generally be trusted, a bit higher than in most Latin American and African countries, but much lower than almost everywhere else.[29] Trust toward public institutions is also weak: Too often, the relation between the state and the citizen is adversarial.

In China as well, plenty of abuse of public goods has taken place. China has taken some action by investigating suspected cases of corruption and severely punishing the perpetrators to deter others. This has not happened in India, where unclear laws too often remain unenforced. There are so many rules and regulations that it is impossible to comply with all of them, many of which are outdated. Safe from the knowledge that they have little risk of getting caught but could potentially make a very good return, people are more likely to ask for bribes in exchange for their services, whether they are tax collectors, police officers, or politicians. Corruption represents a drain on India's economy. What is required is a simplification of most rules and regulations, a more functional judiciary, and sanctions that are commensurate with the crimes committed.

Absent teachers

In 2012, India decided for the first time to participate in the PISA education rankings. The states of Tamil Nadu and Himachal Pradesh, considered national powerhouses when it comes to primary education, were selected for the rankings. The results were not what authorities had expected. India ranked second last in a list of 73 countries, ahead only of Kirghizstan (it did "achieve" the bottom rank in science). The authorities were concerned, not so much by the dismal state of education in the country, but by what they claimed was inadequate methodology in assessing the students. India, they argued, scored badly not because of poor education, but because the questions were not appropriate.[30] The fact that students from every other country that participated in the study were asked the same questions apparently eluded them. It was then decided that India would no longer participate in future rankings (more recently authorities announced their intention to participate again in the next round).

India is a nation of contrasts, and education is no different. Some of the most highly educated people on the planet are Indian, graduating from the best universities and occupying senior positions in various industries. But many others lack access to proper education. 315 million Indians, more than a fifth of total population, remain illiterate.[31] More than half of all students aged 14–18 cannot do simple division.[32] Most children do go to school: Enrollment rates are close to 100 percent. The problem is that too many of them learn very little. In rural areas, a lack of education hinders the ability of farmers to switch from agriculture to other industries with better prospects.

Access to school is not the issue. A vast majority of children live within half a mile of their school.[33] The issue has to do with teachers and the incentives they are given, or lack thereof, to do their job. Teachers in public schools who have no risk of being dismissed and not paid based on their performance have little incentive to work hard or even show up in class. Such incentives may not be required in a high-social-trust society, but they certainly are when social trust is lacking. Teachers in public schools sometimes even take a second job in a private school to earn two salaries. A study observed that a quarter of teachers were absent during unannounced school visits.[34] How can students possibly learn much when faced with such an environment?

Fed up with public schools, more and more parents register their children with private schools despite the higher costs. They prefer to pay for private schools because they know that their children will receive a better education. Private schools perform better because teachers are given an incentive to do their job properly. If they do not show up for class, they are likely to be sanctioned.

Education in India has undeniably progressed over the years: Enrollment and literacy rates, school access to drinking water, and the availability of libraries, toilets, and electricity have all improved.[35] To be fair, providing quality education in a nation as large and diverse as India will always represent a herculean task. But a weak educational system is preventing India's workforce from acquiring the necessary skills to become more productive.

A nation of savers but few exports

Whereas China has led the world in infrastructure investment, modernizing its economy by upgrading its cities and transportation system, India has lagged behind. That is not to say that things have not improved. The financial district in Mumbai is on par with other financial centers around the world. Refurbished airports in the larger cities are more modern than most airports in the US or Europe. India has successfully launched satellites and, in August 2023, became only the fourth nation to land a spacecraft on the moon. But at the same time, the country's fastest train, which embarrassingly broke down during its inaugural trip in February 2019, is 40 percent slower than a high-speed train in China or Japan. Projects are often delayed, sometimes indefinitely.

This is surprising because, similar to China, India is a nation of savers. Despite low average incomes, households save about 20 percent of their income.[b] Overall, the country saves about 30 percent of its GDP, which is substantial by international comparison.[36] As savings make their way into investments, those investments represent about 30 percent of India's GDP, roughly the same portion that the country saves. But, how can the country be investing so much and yet see limited improvement in its infrastructure? Where is all the investment going?

It mostly goes into services, such as telecom, power, and banks. Manufacturers should be investing a lot more and, faced with relatively low domestic consumption, should be focusing on export markets, just like Chinese manufacturers have done. But as we have seen, with few exceptions, they struggle with overreaching regulations that prevent them from growing to a size which would enable them to compete internationally. As they focus on their domestic market, they are unable to generate strong margins to further invest in their production capabilities. Many of them are saddled with debt with little hope of it ever getting repaid.

Nations with high savings rates typically end up with higher net exports as local companies cannot only rely on domestic demand for their products and services. India is an exception: Its people are thrifty and yet the country is a net importer. One reason for this anomaly, as discussed earlier, is the low productivity of the manufacturing and agriculture sectors. Another reason is that the numbers are distorted. A large portion of foreign direct investments come from Indian-controlled companies based in Mauritius and used as funding intermediaries or profit

---

[b] In September 2023, there were alarmist reports in local newspapers about household savings dropping to a 50-year low of 5.1 percent, but this figure only represents financial assets of households; it excludes physical assets. Because of lower mortgage rates, many Indians acquired properties, reducing their financial assets but increasing their physical assets. The combined financial and physical savings of households continue to represent around 20 percent of GDP.

centers. A free trade agreement between the two countries and favorable tax rates have lured Indian businesses to the small island nation. Singapore and Dubai are two other well-known centers where Indian groups have established subsidiaries or sister companies.[37] What this effectively means is that Indian businesses with overseas subsidiaries are generating some of their savings abroad. Another factor at play is remittance from Indians working overseas that represents close to 3 percent of the GDP, one of the highest rates in the world.[38] These add up to overseas savings not captured under domestic savings figures. The country therefore saves more than what the official numbers would suggest and would likely show a positive current account balance if those overseas savings were recorded as domestic savings.

The thriftiness of the Indian population is a testament to the high potential of the country in achieving higher exports and more productive investments at home to modernize its infrastructure. But again, realizing that potential boils down to enacting policies that are conducive to growth. Thriftiness is also under threat because, similar to what is happening in China, young Indians are more willing to spend compared to older generations. Some incur debts to acquire a car or the latest technological gadget, something that was unfathomable to their parents or grandparents. This trend is expected to reduce the nation's savings rate in the years to come, which would in turn reduce the ability of the country to invest and export.

Falling behind China, but for how long?

India's economy has been transformed over the past 30 years, lifting millions out of poverty. It is often compared to China with both countries of roughly equal size and enjoying similar rates of GDP growth. Yet, observers often forget that the Indian population is growing much faster than China's, about three times as fast. So even if India's economy grows at about the same pace as that of China, a Chinese citizen is still getting richer more quickly than his Indian counterpart. GDP per capita is four times higher in China than in India and that gap is not getting any narrower.

There is, however, reason to be optimistic about India's future. Its high potential is primarily driven by a hardworking, young, and inexpensive workforce that, under the right incentives and policies, can only drive productivity higher. A thrifty society should translate into higher investment, better infrastructure, and stronger exports. Endowed with human values conducive to growth, the country needs to push ahead with further liberalization of its manufacturing and agricultural sectors. The government has an important role to play in that process. This requires improving the skills of workers through a stronger education system that provides the right incentives for teachers to perform. The state can also breed national champions to compete with foreign companies. But it needs to stop interfering with domestic market forces. That means allowing a process of creative destruction to run its course by letting companies compete freely with one another, on a level playing field. This has mostly happened in services with results that are clear to everyone. The same needs to happen in manufacturing and agriculture.

Some of this is happening. Significant improvements have been made in the past few years. The most sweeping tax reform since independence, aimed at simplifying the archaic maze of existing sales taxes, has made it easier and cheaper to transport goods within the country and has improved tax collection. A new bankruptcy law is speeding up insolvency proceedings and forcing promoters of struggling businesses to suffer real consequences, preventing them from repurchasing their own company at the expense of creditors. Outdated laws, including one drafted during colonial times which states that any finding in the ground worth as little as 10 rupees belongs to "her Majesty," are finally being scrapped. India's global ranking in terms of ease of doing business (63rd) has improved markedly in recent years, though it remains behind China (31st).[39] A record amount of foreign direct investment has poured into the country. The creation of new businesses is supported by fewer regulations and increased funding. A push to offer government services online and connect rural areas has contributed to India becoming one of the largest and fastest-growing bases of digital users.[40] Not all reforms have been successful. New market-oriented laws in agriculture were proposed in 2020, but had to be repealed a year later due to opposition from farmers wary of competition and eager to preserve their existing privileges. The banknote demonetization of 2016, in which large banknotes were taken out of circulation and replaced by new ones, was poorly executed and failed to curb black money. Upgrades to the network of highways have been delayed, mostly because of land acquisition disputes. One could argue that the pace of reforms is relatively slow. Yet China has often been praised for its gradualist approach to market reforms. Reforming a system takes time in a country as large and diverse as India.

Relatively low production costs present the country with a golden opportunity to replace China as the manufacturing center of the world now that China, faced with rising labor costs, focuses increasingly on more innovative and higher value-added products. The services sector will continue to grow, but it cannot by itself cater to the needs of the entire economy; in particular, it cannot provide jobs to the millions of young Indians entering the job market every year. As India aspires to catch up with China, further market reforms in manufacturing and agriculture, as well as a strong stance against corruption and improvements in the education sector, will be essential for the country to fully realize its enormous potential.

Chapter 6

Japan

I n the 1980s, it seemed Japan had invented a superior economic model. The country was booming: Japanese manufacturers were flooding international markets with innovative, affordable, and high-quality products. Some had gone on an overseas acquisition spree, purchasing the likes of tire producer Firestone (by Bridgestone) or filmmaker Columbia Pictures (by Sony), eliciting fears among the western world that Japan was taking over. Unwavering optimism in Japan and financial deregulation led to surging property prices as banks lent freely, culminating in the oft-cited and somewhat exaggerated observation that the grounds of the Imperial Palace in Tokyo were worth more than the entire real estate of California. Many in Japan felt that this era would go on forever, that Japanese companies would generate record profits on a permanent basis, and that stock and property prices could only go up. The country had lost the war, but was winning the economic battle. Even those who believed that the ongoing exuberance would at some point come to an end were convinced that the Japanese government would intervene to ensure that, using a contemporary expression, the music would not stop.

Then the music stopped and the bubble burst. What caused the bubble to burst (an appreciating yen, a new consumption tax, an overly accommodative monetary policy) is irrelevant: The bubble would have burst anyway, sooner or later. This scenario of boom and bust, where people become overconfident and then start to panic, has occurred time and time again, most recently during the financial crisis of 2008. But the fundamental difference between Japan and other bubbles is that after a few years of stagnation, people normally regain their optimism and the economy rebounds. Yet in Japan, this has not happened: Despite short-lived periods of growth following the crisis, the country never really recovered from the highs of the 1980s, entering a series of "lost decades" characterized by anemic growth, stagnant wages, and minimal inflation. GDP per person, adjusted for inflation and currency movements, increased by just 20 percent in the 30 years since 1990, or less than one percent of real growth each year.[1] Leading Japanese manufacturers in consumer electronics, semiconductors, or machine tools have all lost global market share. Only a handful of new Japanese companies have emerged over the past 30 years. Starting in 2012, the reforms undertaken by the government of the late Shinzo Abe, the most sweeping in decades, yielded some result, but not quite what had been hoped for. Wages are not increasing despite record low unemployment. Japan's main stock market index only recently exceeded the record it had set in 1989.[2]

With the benefit of hindsight, Japan could have been more responsive in the years that followed 1989: Its central bank was slow to react, debt levels kept on piling up, and insolvent firms were kept alive artificially. Yet none of these factors can explain why Japan never returned to sustainable growth over such a long period of time and after so many attempts to spur growth. We argue that the main reason Japan has found itself in this predicament for the past 30 years is the *lost ability of its people to take risks*. Too much risk was taken during the boom years, but after the bubble burst, the Japanese have become extremely risk-averse and have remained so ever since.

Turning inward

It starts from a young age: Children are told off as soon as their behavior is considered bad or dangerous, even for trivial matters that would be considered perfectly acceptable in other societies. Japanese kids may grow up with a fear of doing something wrong and carry that fear throughout their lives. Only 6 percent of Japan's household assets are invested in stocks versus 33 percent in the US and 15 percent in Europe. Risk aversion manifests itself even in unlikely settings. Professional baseball teams in Japan bunt twice as often as those in the US (in baseball, a bunt is a ball tapped slowly with the bat, often done in an attempt to advance a runner and is thus considered less risky than swinging at the ball).[3]

Highly risk-averse Japanese are unwilling to spend their income. According to surveys, only 5 percent of Japanese people would consider increasing their spending in the following year.[4] Consumption as a proportion of the GDP did increase since 1990, but the data are distorted by demographic factors: Working-age Japanese continue to save a large portion of their income, probably as much as they did since the early 1990s.[5] Those who are *reluctantly* increasing consumption figures (again as a proportion of national income) are retirees, who would rather save up but are unable to do so. The Japanese are a thrifty population, yet the savings rate has decreased over the years, from 35 percent in the 1990s to 28 percent in 2022.[6] Japanese workers continue to save a high portion of their income, but an increasing number of retirees end up with negative savings rates, not because they wish to spend more, but because their income during retirement does not cover their basic expenses. As the population becomes older, the savings rate of households decreases further.

The same is true of Japanese companies, which have been hoarding large quantities of cash and have shown little interest in investing in new technologies or expanding overseas. They have also so far been unwilling to increase wages, citing uncertain prospects. This may seem odd. In a country that heavily restrains access to foreign workers, where many local workers are retiring, fewer babies are born, and students graduate at an older age, there are plenty of jobs available. Unemployment figures are at record lows. In most countries, employees would take advantage of that situation by negotiating a higher pay or shifting employers. But, in Japan, real wages have remained stagnant for the past 20 years.

It turns out that the job market in Japan is much less dynamic compared to many other high-income countries. The job-for-life system, threatened by retrenchments in the 1990s, remains the expectation for most workers. Many firms continue the long-standing practice of hiring mostly new graduates and employing them until they retire. In such a system, workers develop a strong bond with their employer over the years. Job security in risk-averse Japan is much more highly valued than wage increases. Workers favor harmony and unity with their colleagues over their personal interests, even if that comes at the expense of individual achievement. Those who break that corporate harmony by seeking work elsewhere may be chastised, accused of abandoning their employer and colleagues. Those few workers who do leave their job very rarely do so because they were unhappy with their wages. When they apply for a new role, compensation may not even be mentioned, let alone negotiated. Such concepts may seem alien to the non-Japanese, but they play an important role in shaping the local workplace.

An important structural change since the mid-1990s has been the increased reliance on "non-regular" or temporary workers, which now make up more than a third of the workforce. Firms faced with declining productivity are increasingly relying on non-regular workers to reduce labor costs when activity slows down. Those jobs often require few qualifications, are mostly filled by women or retirees, and earn much less for the same amount of work compared to "regular" workers.

The Japanese are becoming increasingly insular, turning themselves away from the outside world. Only 23 percent of Japanese hold a passport, a proportion that has been in regular decline over the years and despite the fact that few countries require Japanese travelers to acquire a visa.[7] Some become so insular that even stepping out of their home is a step too far: More than a million working-age Japanese are believed to be completely withdrawn from society, a trend that the COVID-19 pandemic has accentuated.[8] A study ranked Japan 37th out of 80 countries for English language ability.[9] The country has few native English teachers as a result of its very strict immigration policy. Foreign movies are dubbed, not subtitled. There are a few exceptions: Rakuten, often referred to as the Amazon of Japan and perhaps better known around the world as the official sponsor of Barcelona Football Club until 2022, made English its primary office communication language.[10] English classes may be mandatory in schools, but proficiency in the language remains elusive as students have little interest in learning the language except to pass high school and university exams. Since they do not expect to interact with people in other nations, they see little point in learning a new language.

Productivity in decline

Although the economy is predominantly driven by market forces, a lack of innovation and an inability for companies to invest in risky projects have stifled dynamism in the Japanese corporate world. But there are also other factors hampering an effective process of creative destruction and ultimately higher productivity. One is that the Japanese business model is based on long-term relations. Most companies will deal with the same suppliers and buyers throughout and expect the same loyalty from their counterparts. This results in a lack of competition between companies operating within the same industry. Local companies are sheltered in their domestic market because foreign competitors face high barriers to entry, both formal and informal ones. As a result, local firms become complacent and increasingly struggle to compete when venturing outside of Japan.

Another factor hindering domestic competition is the bailout of struggling and sometimes insolvent "zombie" companies by Japanese banks. This creates a host of negative outcomes: unfair advantages over competitors; misallocation of credit with funding going to zombie companies instead of healthier ones; little incentive for zombie firms to improve on their situation knowing that they will be supported by the banks or the government no matter what; and reduced opportunities for new companies to enter the market. Although the long-term consequences of those actions are clear, things are unlikely to change. The government, in conjunction with local banks, will almost never allow a large Japanese company to go bankrupt and face the prospect of thousands of jobs lost.

Heavy regulation, bureaucracy, and red tape are other issues, particularly in the services sector that makes up a majority of the national income. Japanese services companies are only half as productive as their US counterparts and have barely shown any improvement since 1990.[11] There are countless stories of mismanagement and inefficiencies plaguing the system. In *The Blue-Eyed Salaryman*, Irishman Niall Murtagh, who worked for 14 years at Mitsubishi, describes the inner workings of the Japanese corporate world, with numerous reports drafted but never reviewed by anyone, innovative ideas constantly shunned, and promotions based solely on age rather than merit.[12] While such anecdotes are not uncommon in other countries, they tend to be exacerbated in Japan, where the smallest decision requires senior managerial approval.

Still a very prosperous nation

Although Japan has gone through a prolonged period of slow growth, largely because of the risk aversion of its people, the country remains highly developed, with a GDP per capita roughly the same as that of the United Kingdom. This is clear to anyone visiting Japan.

Prosperity has been primarily achieved through a market economy and the fact that the Japanese are undeniably hardworking, with the ability to come together and work the hardest in the face of adversity, as demonstrated by how quickly and methodically the nation has been rebuilt in the aftermath of national disasters, such as World War II, the Kobe earthquake of 1995, or the Fukushima nuclear accident of 2011. *Gaman*, a term that many Japanese commonly associate with, refers to the ability to persevere with patience and dignity despite the difficulties that life may bring. At the workplace, employees clock up some of the longest working hours in the world, many more than what employment contracts officially state. Most workers take great pride in their work and are grateful toward their employer for having hired them and for looking after them. Sometimes, this goes too far: About 100 deaths are reported every year because of overwork.[13] Besides, working long hours does not make workers more productive. Productivity growth has been steadily declining not only because of a lack of innovation and excessive bureaucracy but also because Japanese workers can spend long hours in the office not doing much in a country where employers are reluctant to lay off staff and where there is significant peer pressure to stay in the office even when the work is completed.

Hard work often leads to strong performance at school, and Japan is no exception. Education is of an excellent standard, with the country ranking highly in PISA tests, higher than the OECD average in mathematics, science, and reading.[14] Teachers are well trained and highly respected by both students and parents. They will perform to the best of their abilities without the need for monitoring or financial incentives. Top Japanese universities also perform well in international rankings. Although more could be done to teach English, overall, the Japanese workforce is undeniably a highly educated one.

Japan also does well when it comes to corruption, ranked as the 18th least corrupt country in the world by Transparency International. This is underpinned by a relatively high level of social trust: 34 percent of Japanese believe that most people can be trusted, a level that has not dropped since 1990.[15] This is comparable to levels seen in the US or Germany. Relations between companies are based on trust, more so than on legal documentation. Cases of tax dodging or abuse of social benefits are rare: Even if people knew they could get away with it, they would still not proceed accordingly because such behavior goes against their values. A strong sense of ethics and togetherness features prominently in Japanese culture: Individuals would feel ashamed to take advantage of a system that benefits the collective. The state is seen as a legitimate redistributor of wealth, which has contributed to a society that is much more equal than many others, with senior executives earning far less than their counterparts in the US or the UK, and poorer sections of the population benefiting from subsidized access to a strong universal health-care system.

Some sectors are doing better than others. The automotive industry has so far bucked the trend of a reduced global presence and slow growth. Employing close to ten percent of the country's workforce and representing a fifth of all manufactured exports, Japanese carmakers capitalized on the superior technology and processes that allowed them to become market leaders in the 1970s and 1980s.[16] Most of them already had a sizable presence outside Japan before the 1990 crisis, not only so that they could be closer to their main destination markets but also to escape higher costs at home and rising protectionism in the US. Their vehicles have proven very popular with growing middle classes in emerging markets, who are attracted to affordable, efficient, and high-quality Japanese models and tend to shun more expensive western brands.

But, the ability of Japanese carmakers to stay ahead of the curve post-1990 was not the result of audacious and visionary decisions made in corporate boardrooms. The decision to manufacture hybrid models in the mid-1990s was made to comply with more stringent environmental regulations, in particular the Low-Emissions Vehicle Program in California, among the world's largest car markets. The Toyota Prius, launched in 1997, was not an immediate success, but a complete redesign in the early 2000s made it one of the most successful hybrid models.

Can Japan replicate the hybrid success with electric vehicles (EVs)? Similar to hybrids, the foray into EVs was more of an accident than a concerted effort by local carmakers. It started from an unlikely source. As an engineer working for TEPCO, Japan's largest electricity and nuclear energy provider, Takafumi Anegawa was keen to reduce Japan's reliance on imported energy. He saw EVs as the perfect solution and devoted himself to improving EV technology in the early 2000s, at a time when Toyota and a few other Japanese carmakers were heavily focused on hybrids. Anegawa is not a typical risk-averse citizen. When he believes in an idea, he forges ahead with it. He quotes JFK, "We should go to the moon because it is difficult, not because it's easy," and describes himself as "a very strange guy." His colleagues call him "crazy Anegawa." In 2002, he managed to convince METI, the powerful ministry of economy, trade, and industry that plays an important role in shaping the country's industrial policy, to promote EVs by offering generous subsidies. The problem though was that no car manufacturer was interested. It would take a few more years for two smaller car manufacturers, Mitsubishi and Subaru, to seriously explore EVs' potential. But it was Nissan, the third largest Japanese carmaker helmed at the time by a non-Japanese, that would produce EVs on a much larger scale with its LEAF model.[17]

Despite Nissan's success, few other Japanese carmakers have invested in EVs and even Nissan seems to have run out of steam. A lack of risk-taking prevents most manufacturers from investing in new technologies, preferring instead to improve existing technologies. There is a real risk that Japanese automakers will be left behind and ultimately suffer the same fate as consumer electronics firms.[18]

Funding the needs of an aging population

Japan's pension system is coming under increased financial strain, costing the government more each year as the population becomes older. People are living longer and too few babies are born. The population is shrinking rapidly, with 500,000 *more* Japanese passing away every year than babies being born.[19] This is a global trend in developed countries, but is exacerbated in Japan because of a high life expectancy, low fertility rate, and the fact that the country has remained mostly closed to immigration. The retirement age urgently needs to be raised, but that is happening much too timidly. Fewer workers and more retirees are creating a headache for government budget officials. In large part because of a graying population, the government spends a lot more than what it earns: Its annual deficit, expressed as a percentage of GDP, has been above 3 percent for over a decade.[20] Expenses will continue to increase as more and more Japanese go into retirement.

To remedy the situation, the government has sought to increase taxes and incur more debt. Increasing taxes (in the form of higher value-added taxes) in an economy already struggling with weak demand is unlikely to succeed, as people will spend ever less. As for debt, Japan has the highest public debt in the world relative to GDP (even Greece carried less public debt at the height of its crisis). Yet this has not resulted in a major crisis and Japan remains a very safe and trustworthy creditor. There are good reasons for that. Almost half of that debt is owned by the central bank and other governmental agencies. Only around 10 percent is owned by foreigners; if they were to withdraw their support, this is unlikely to have much of an impact, unlike what happened in Thailand in 1997 or Greece in 2010. The cost of servicing public debt remains very low, with interest rates close to zero or in negative territory.

Over the last decade, Japan's central bank has purchased vast quantities of government debt. The amount of money created through that process has been unprecedented. In other countries and under normal circumstances, actions on such a scale would have led to price inflation and possibly asset bubbles. But not in Japan. Prices for goods and services have remained stubbornly low because a significant portion of all that newly created money ends up getting trapped with banks and large corporations. Banks are unwilling to lend more and businesses are unwilling to invest more because they are too risk-averse to do so (inflation did go up in 2023, but this was entirely due to the higher cost of imports driven by a much stronger US dollar and more expensive imported goods, not the result of any domestic factor). It all comes back to the idea that risk aversion is the main reason for Japan's paltry economic performance.

Abe to the rescue

After years of ineffective public policy and a string of prime ministers, Shinzo Abe's second term in office started in 2012, during which he enacted a series of bold reforms focused on three "arrows": large asset purchases by the central bank, increased government spending, including infrastructure projects, and structural reforms, all aimed at depreciating the yen, raising inflation and wages, and ultimately spurring growth. Initially, the arrows seemed to pay off, especially the first one: The yen depreciated by 25 percent within a year, boosting Japanese exports and increasing GDP. But after a decade, those policies have run out of steam: Wages have not picked up and growth remains anemic. An ill-advised decision to raise the consumption tax in 2014 and again in 2019 did little to help.

Despite those setbacks, there have been significant achievements. Japan joined the Trans-Pacific Partnership, a free trade agreement between nations across the Pacific Ocean. The agriculture and energy sectors have been liberalized to some extent. Female employment has reached record levels due to new gender equity laws, the expansion of childcare programs, and the requirement for large companies to publish reports of their progress in promoting women managers. Progress has also been made in promoting external directors on corporate boards, the establishment of special economic zones with lower taxes, and increasing the allocation to risky assets for public pension funds. There are also plans to increase the number of overseas Japanese students, promote the learning of English, reduce the wage gap between regular and non-regular workers, and establish a fund to stimulate the development of start-ups.

Drastic action needed

Those reforms broadly go in the right direction. But they have so far not yielded much result. Japan's economy has been "stuck in time" for three decades. Too many companies have become complacent, relying on their historical network of commercial partners, safe in the knowledge that no new company, local or foreign, will disrupt their operations and that banks are likely to continue supporting them if they run into difficulties. The job market is equally muted, with few workers willing to switch between employers and unable to press for higher wages. As the economy moves at an ever-slower pace, Japanese companies are being left behind, unable to compete with more efficient US, Chinese, or Korean competitors.

This evolution is an unfortunate one given Japan's potential. The combination of a hardworking, thrifty, trusting, and well-educated population in conjunction with a market economy is a recipe for sustained economic growth. That was certainly true for half a century following the end of the war. If it were not for the country's extreme risk aversion, Japan would in all likelihood have continued on that growth path and become one of the most prosperous nations on earth. Risk aversion is here to stay unless it can be alleviated by drastic measures that force people and companies to change their behavior. The government has taken bold action in recent years and should be commended for it. It, however, would need to go a step further for the Japanese economy to fulfill its potential.

The rise of the Chinese economy is often seen as a threat, producing higher-value products that compete with Japanese exports. But as we have argued in the case of Singapore, it also represents an opportunity as Chinese consumers have become the main growth driver of their economy, increasingly attracted to more valuable goods and services and with a purchasing power to match that appetite. India, Southeast Asia, and much of Africa are going through similar trends with a growing middle class that desires cars, phones, home appliances, and other products. Japan should capitalize on its unique know-how to take advantage of those opportunities. This is, however, unlikely to happen. The country may well experience several more lost decades.

Chapter 7

Nigeria

The neighborhood of Sanyuanli, located in the southern Chinese city of Guangzhou, contains many wholesale markets close to the city's main railway station. First-time visitors to those markets, in search of affordable clothing, perfumes, or other counterfeit products, will be surprised by the people they encounter. Most are Chinese-owned shops, often with poorly translated names, such as "Europe More Rat Dress-shop" or "Altogether Wins Clothing Firms." But in many of those markets, up to a fifth of all shops are manned by Africans. The most commonly used language, Igbo, is one that most visitors would never have heard of.

Prior to COVID-19, an estimated 15,000–20,000 Africans worked in Guangzhou, the largest African community in Asia. They are middlemen (few women are involved), purchasing clothes, handbags, shoes, cosmetics, jewelry, and electronics from Chinese suppliers and shipping them to Africa. Those traders act as an interface between two worlds that have become two of the biggest global trends: The "factory of the world" in Southeast China that mass-produces cheap but functional products and a growing African middle class eager to consume those goods.

Initially, the China–Africa trade for consumer goods was handled exclusively by the Chinese: Chinese suppliers shipping goods to Chinese migrants who had set up shops in various African countries. But starting in the late 1990s, a handful of brave West Africans moved to Guangzhou, sensing an opportunity to strike it rich by gaining a share of this lucrative trade. Several of their compatriots have since followed in their footsteps. African traders have several advantages over Chinese traders: closer ties to retailers, warehouse operators, and customs authorities in Africa and a better understanding of end-buyers. But you will find very few *East* African traders in Guangzhou. An overwhelming majority of traders from Africa are Nigerians, more specifically Igbo Nigerians, one of the biggest ethnic groups in the country.

Opportunities exist, but this is a business fraught with risks and dangers, where only the best traders succeed. Many of them fail and leave Guangzhou within a year of their arrival. Their status in the city is precarious: Most will enter China with a business visa valid for a few months; extending it is complicated and many traders end up overstaying, at the risk of repatriation to their home country if they get caught in a police raid. The products they sell are mostly counterfeits. As such, most of their activities are informal. They often use a different name, sub-rent their shop instead of renting it under their name, and do not hold a local bank account. African traders also have to adapt to a very different culture and a language that they do not understand (interpreters are in high demand). They face heavy discrimination because of the color of their skin, something that was exacerbated during COVID-19 when many landlords ejected them from their apartments and several restaurants refused to serve them.

Traders face other risks. Those involved in the clothing business may be caught caught unawares if cotton prices go up and they have already agreed to sales terms with their buyers before locking in purchase terms with their suppliers. Currency fluctuations are another concern: If the Chinese renminbi appreciates against the Nigerian naira or the US dollar, the trader will lose out, because he will need more nairas or US dollars to convert into renminbis to pay his suppliers. Then there are changing consumer trends, such as clothes that go out of fashion, which can leave a trader with a large stock of unsold clothes. Sometimes, traders get cheated by their Chinese suppliers, receiving badly dyed clothes which lose their colors after being washed.

Changing fashion trends also represent an opportunity, as it increases demand for new clothes. In fact, clothing is where the largest profits can be made. It is easier to trade counterfeit clothes than counterfeit cosmetics or electronics. Everyone along the supply chain tries to capture the biggest margins, from cotton producers, textile factories, and clothes factories to wholesale markets in China and retailers in Africa. Some traders move up the value chain, purchasing directly from textile factories or even acquiring local factories, allowing them to produce their own designs. Most of their profits are saved to expand their business. The best way to increase margins is to trade more best-selling items, thereby achieving economies of scale by reducing the cost of each item sold. But betting everything on a few items can be dangerous: Supplies may become more expensive or the items may go out of fashion. The best traders are able to achieve a balance between specializing in the best-selling products and keeping a large enough range of products to trade. During periods when African economies perform poorly, established traders become consultants, teaching the tricks of the trade to newcomers for a fee, and also collecting a fee from Chinese factories for introducing them to new customers.

All this requires a lot of ingenuity. Sometimes, that ingenuity is used for illegal purposes. It is not uncommon for customs officers to be bribed, especially in Nigeria where textile imports are illegal. Clothing items are officially registered as non-textile imports and customs officers are paid to look away. Security guards at the entrance of apartments housing African traders are given cash to warn the traders whenever a police raid is underway, giving them sufficient time to escape. All transactions are settled in cash. To send over large amounts of cash from Africa to China, traders use the services of flight attendants, who collect the funds when they fly out and deliver them to their contact upon landing in China. A minority of traders have been involved in drug dealing or the trading of endangered species. Bus fares in Guangzhou are rarely paid for by the traders. Buses use an electronic reader where a card must be tapped. Traders bypass it by using a fake card to tap (or a real one with no cash balance) and a small whistle hidden in their pocket that imitates the sound of the reader machine.

That was all before the COVID-19 pandemic. Less than 5,000 African traders are estimated to remain in Guangzhou, although that number should rise again with the lifting of pandemic restrictions.[1] Those who flew out of China could not return. Those who remained were subject to much closer scrutiny, asked to show identity papers when entering buildings or different districts, and often repatriated if caught. The few who stayed on are often those who have married Chinese women and fathered a child with a Chinese passport, making their local situation slightly less precarious. The cutthroat competition, not just from the Chinese but also from other Africans, meant that only the best traders were able to make it. A vast majority of traders who remained were Igbo, who were better often able to scale up their operations compared to their fellow Africans. Their success in Guangzhou against all odds was achieved because of their ingenuity, their ability to establish strong connections, and, above all, their willingness to work hard.[2]

A troubled past

When most of us think of Nigeria, the first thing that comes to mind is probably Internet scams, where supposedly high-ranking officials or widows of dictators promise to transfer millions of dollars against an initial fee. The kidnapping of young girls or summary executions by religious extremists has also made the headlines in recent years.

We were told by work colleagues that first-time visitors to Lagos should memorize the photo of their driver beforehand to minimize the risk of getting kidnapped by someone with access to the flight's passenger manifest and holding a sign with the passenger's name on it. Whatever that first image may be, it is usually not a glamorous one. Few would have heard of Nigeria's large film industry, its wide range of yam- and cassava-based dishes, the role of Lagos as the fashion and financial capital for West Africa, or the vibrant energy of its people.

One thing that sets Nigeria apart is the size of its population. Its 225 million people make it by far the most populated African nation despite a land size that is only the 14th largest on the continent (the second and third most populated African nations, Ethiopia and Egypt, have larger land sizes but their populations are 125 and 110 million, respectively). In 2019, Nigeria overtook South Africa to become Africa's largest economy. Economic figures are not the most reliable: In 2014, Nigerian statisticians included new sectors, such as telecommunications, retail, and the film industry, in their GDP calculations, which increased by 90 percent as a result. Still, Nigeria is an economic heavyweight.

The economy may be large, but given the size of its population, most people remain poor. The GDP per capita is similar to that of neighboring countries, but is much lower compared to the likes of South Africa, Egypt, or Botswana. According to the World Bank, 40 percent of Nigerians (83 million people) live below the poverty line, defined as less than $1.90 a day, while another 25 percent (53 million) are vulnerable.[3] But Nigeria is also home to Africa's richest man, a small number of elite politicians and industrialists who have benefited greatly from oil revenues, and a small but growing middle class. Oil is a major contributor to Nigeria's economy, accounting for 80 percent of exports and half of all government revenues, although it represents less than 10 percent of GDP.[4]

All these numbers, provided at the national level, hide important disparities within the country that, left ignored, can never provide a true reflection of the dynamics of Nigerian society. This is a very diverse nation, home to more than 250 tribes, each with their own language and culture. The three main ones are the Hausa–Fulani in the north, the Yoruba in the southwest, and the Igbo in the southeast. The Hausa–Fulani are predominantly Muslim, whereas the Yoruba and Igbo are mainly Christian.

Several conflicts have taken place between the tribes over the years. The southeastern states with an Igbo majority, the third largest tribe with about 40 million people, declared independence in 1967 and proclaimed themselves the Republic of Biafra, provoking government forces into a deadly conflict. The Nigerian Civil War, also known as the Biafran War, lasted three years, during which both sides committed atrocities. More than a million civilians died, mostly on the Biafran side and mostly due to starvation, after the blockade of the key coastal city of Port Harcourt. Government forces eventually prevailed, beginning a long and delicate reconciliation process.

The Igbo lost almost everything in the war. Their savings became worthless. Each adult bank account holder in the former Biafra received the equivalent of 400 US dollars (at current rates) from the government in exchange for their Biafran pounds, whatever the amount of cash they had in the bank. They became heavily discriminated against when applying for jobs or participating in politics (to this day, no Igbo has ever become Nigerian president). According to the account of a local writer, "Thoroughly demoralized, psychologically disoriented, materially impoverished and politically marooned, their future appeared permanently blighted. To be Igbo became taboo, and some Igbo groups attempted to hide Igbo identity by disguising their Igbo name."[5]

They had lost most of their belongings, but they retained something even more important — their values. And among those values is a belief in hard work and that hard work will eventually lead to success. And it did.

Soiled hands lead to oily mouth[a]

From a very young age, Igbo children are taught about the importance of hard work, resilience, honesty, and also property and money. Upward mobility and a high social status are considered some of the most important goals in life. Those who are unable to become financially independent and have to rely on relatives and friends for their livelihood because of a perceived lack of hard work tend to be looked down upon. An Igbo who dies poor does not deserve a place among the ancestors.[6] Even some of the common Igbo names reflect this pursuit of materialistic gain, such as Ogbenyeanu ("to be married not by the poor"), Egodi ("there is money"), or Egoamaka ("money is good").

Success in Igbo culture can only come from an individual's efforts, not the actions of the community or any form of inheritance. In Chinua Achebe's *Things Fall Apart*, one of the most famous novels written by an African writer, published in 1958, Okonkwo, the main protagonist, works as hard as he can to rise above his peers and distance himself from his father's idleness and failures in life. Everyone is expected to do their part to ensure the continued prosperity of the community. Achebe further commented many decades after his first novel that "Igbo culture being individualistic and highly competitive, gave the Igbo man an unquestioned advantage over his compatriots in securing credentials or advancement in Nigerian society."[7]

Not only are the Igbo hardworking, they are also risk-takers. Entrepreneurship is a common career path for many Igbo, in Nigeria and abroad. Not many people would leave their homeland to go to Guangzhou, arriving with few belongings and living in precarious conditions in a vastly different cultural setting. They see opportunities where most see threats. If it does not work out, they will try their luck elsewhere. The more they try, the likelier they are to succeed.

---

[a] Igbo proverb that means "hard work leads to success."

Through their hard work and entrepreneurship, the Igbo dominate Nigeria's economic landscape. When the country acquired its independence from the British in 1960, the Igbo were already dominating commerce and several parts of the public sector, not only in states with an Igbo majority but also in Lagos and other financial and trading centers (Lagos is the economic capital of Nigeria; Abuja in the center of the country became the political capital in 1991).[8] After the war, deprived of their assets, the Igbo became one of the poorest ethnic groups in Nigeria. But they gradually rebuilt their wealth, as have other industrious societies before them. A majority of Nigeria's companies are owned and managed by the Igbo.[9] As Achebe once put it, "Igbo ostracization is one of the main reasons for the country's continued backwardness."[10]

If we compare the GDP per capita of the 36 Nigerian states and the federal capital, significant differences exist along ethnic lines. The northern states (previously known as Northern Nigeria) lag behind their southern counterparts: The 19 northern states are among the 23 poorest ones, and not a single northern state is among the top 10 richest ones. The absence of oil and sea access in the north, as well as less arable land for cultivation, provides a partial explanation for those numbers. Indeed, most of the richest states are oil-producing coastal states. But consider the five states with an Igbo majority. None of them produces significant quantities of oil and none has sea access.[11] Yet they rank 3rd, 9th, 12th, 15rd, and 34th in terms of GDP per capita.[12] The Igbo enjoy standards of living far higher than those in the northern states, despite losing all their possessions half a century ago. In the US, Americans of Nigerian descent, about half of whom are estimated to be Igbo, earn more than most other ethnic groups and about the same as White Americans.[13]

The achievements of the Igbo are also reflected in their much higher educational attainments. Results for the standard secondary school exams show that, each year, the five states with an Igbo majority all rank in the top ten, with the state of Abia coming in first most years. This is followed by states in the southeast and southwest. The northern states perform much more poorly.[14] According to the World Bank, Nigeria has an average literacy rate of 62 percent, but this figure again masks big differences. Whereas Igbo states have a literacy rate above 90 percent, many of the northern states struggle with a rate of less than 10 percent. This is not a matter of funding. The northern states have received much more government funding to educate their people compared to the southern states, relative to the size of their populations.[15] It is a matter of hard work, a rejection in the northern states of what some local leaders consider western education, and the political instability that has marred the region in recent times. As for the Yoruba in the southwest, their levels of educational attainments also lag behind those of the Igbo, despite similar standards of living.

The Igbo Apprenticeship System (IAS)

The success of the Igbo is beginning to attract international attention. Yet their success has often been attributed not to their values but to the Igbo Apprenticeship System (IAS), which has recently received coverage in western media and was made into one of Harvard Business School's famous case studies. "Implement the IAS in other societies," the story goes, "and they, too, will experience strong economic growth just as the Igbo have."

What is the IAS? It is a system whereby secondary school or university graduates follow a mentor into a specific entrepreneurial venture to learn how a business operates, for a period of up to 8 years. Only boys take part (most families would be reluctant to have their daughters spend several years with a male mentor). The apprentice receives no pay throughout the apprenticeship; only food, housing, and clothing are provided. At the end of the apprenticeship, the mentor is expected to "reward" his apprentice by transferring a lump sum of money to him, providing a loan, or, in some cases, ceding part or all of his business to him. The apprentice is then on his own. Throughout the apprenticeship, the mentor sets the rules which the apprentice is expected to follow.

The system is sometimes abused. Apprentices may be exploited as free labor, learning little of use during the process. Mentors have at times accused their apprentices of various wrongdoings toward the end of their apprenticeship to avoid rewarding them. No written contract is entered into: Agreements are all verbal, making it difficult for apprentices to defend their rights. The mentor and the apprentice are often related; better-connected young graduates are more likely to take part. But over-all, the IAS has benefited many young Igbo, preparing them well for the world of business and contributing to a more entrepreneurial society. The IAS provides them with an opportunity to secure a job in a country where more than a third of those below the age of 35 are officially unemployed.

It would however be a mistake to attribute the economic success of the Igbo to the apprenticeship system. If other societies were to adopt the same system, they will be disappointed by the results because they will have failed to consider the values that the Igbo identify with, in particular hard work. The IAS was formally implemented after the war; it cannot by itself account for the economic success of the Igbo prior to it. It has contributed to the success of the Igbo, but it is not the main reason behind it.

Poverty capital of the world

Given the economic success of the Igbo, one may wonder why Nigeria's economy as a whole has not performed better. Nigeria holds the unenviable top rank as the country with the most people living in extreme poverty.[16] Part of the reason is that the Igbo only represent 20 percent of all Nigerians, with many of its brightest emigrating from a country where opportunities are more limited and where their voices are not represented at the higher levels of politics. More than half of Nigerians hail from northern states and lack the industriousness of the Igbo and other southern tribes necessary to improve their standards of living. Better policies would help, but even then, the north will always lag behind the south. No amount of funding, from the government or from elsewhere, will change that.

The other reason why Nigeria has been unable to grow further is that its economy has been mismanaged since at least the early 1980s. Various dictators and elected leaders, all promising an end to corruption, have instead embraced it and personally benefited from it. Some of the ministers in the first Nigeria government in the early 1960s were nicknamed the "ten-percenters" in reference to the cut they collected for each contract they approved. Perhaps the best-known case is of Sani Abacha, who ruled Nigeria from 1993 to 1998, transferring more than a billion dollars of taxpayer money to his personal Swiss bank accounts. As is unfortunately the case in many African countries blessed (or cursed) with natural resources, revenue from Nigerian oil only benefits a small elite. Negligible tax is collected in a country with a large informal sector: The tax-to-GDP ratio stands at 6 percent, lower than in most other African countries. The World Bank ranks Nigeria 159th out of 190 countries in its ease of paying taxes (the much better governed Botswana is 59th).[17]

Nigeria's reputation for corruption is well deserved. The country ranks 150th on Transparency International's Corruption Perceptions Index. Other nearby coastal countries rank better: Ghana and Benin are both 72nd, Ivory Coast 99th, Togo 130th, and Cameroon 142nd. The endemic levels of corruption in Nigeria are to a large extent the result of Nigerians not trusting each other. In the latest Afrobarometer survey, more than 9 out of 10 Nigerians believe that "you must be very careful when dealing with people." Only 7 percent feel that most people can be trusted.[18] Nigerian society has had to endure multiple upheavals that have reduced trust over the course of its history. The slave trade affected Nigeria particularly badly. Out of 12.5 million slaves shipped to the

Americas, 3.5 million came from Nigeria.[19] Slavery had been practiced among the Igbo, but the Atlantic slave trade took it to a very different order of magnitude. As people were tricked or kidnapped into slavery by relatives and other contacts, this created a deep distrust among them. The British colonization of Nigeria, from the mid-nineteenth century to 1960, led to a further loss of identity. The wide ethnic diversity of the country has also made people less trusting of each other, especially after the deadly conflicts of the 1960s. And, of course, the various administrations that have governed Nigeria in the past decades also bear responsibility. With levels of trust unlikely to recover any time soon and no real willingness or ability to seriously crack down on corruption, Nigeria will remain a deeply corrupt state.

Other factors have contributed to low economic performance. Political instability is one. While the last few administrations have been democratically elected, ensuring a smooth transfer of power, a welcome change from the numerous coups in the 1980s and 1990s, various insurgencies are hampering progress, such as separatist Igbo movements, insurgencies in the Niger delta, and religious fundamentalism in the north. The monetary policy has also been far from adequate, leading to several bouts of high inflation and devaluations. Many have lost trust in the highly volatile local currency and are using US dollars instead. The legal system is a complicated one, comprising three very different structures: tribal, British-inherited, and Islamic. Despite Igbo entrepreneurship, Nigeria ranks 131st in the world in the ease of doing business. More than half of all Nigerians wish to emigrate.[20] Clearly, there is room for improvement.

Diverse but united

In this chapter, we have focused heavily on Nigeria's different ethnic groups, in particular the Igbo. This is somewhat unfair to other large ethnic groups such as the Hausa or the Yoruba. Our intent was twofold.

Understanding the values of the different ethnic groups that compose Nigeria is key to assess its current economic situation and how this may evolve going forward. But we also focused on the Igbo because we see the community as an important sign of hope for the country and for an entire continent that was once labeled "hopeless" by The Economist magazine two decades ago. The success of the Igbo, in Nigeria and elsewhere, provides evidence that an industrious people willing to take risks have the potential to become highly prosperous, even after a deadly conflict that left them with almost nothing. They are not alone in Africa. The Ashanti (also known as Asante), renowned for their hard work, their risk-taking, and their access to valuable commodities, form the richest tribe in Ghana. Ghanaian Americans, just like Nigerian Americans, are among the richest ethnic groups in the US.[21] If more in Africa could adopt the same values and if their leaders were to adopt the right policies, this would be a game changer for the continent.

We may also have given the impression of a deeply divided Nigeria. Despite isolated incidents, a vast majority of Nigerians have reconciled since the Civil War and learnt to live together. Surveys show that a majority of Nigerians value diverse communities, identify equally with their ethnicity and nationality, and believe there is more that unites Nigerians as one people than divides them. Nine in ten citizens are said to be tolerant of people from different religions, ethnic groups, nationalities, and political parties.[22] Today, Lagos is a modern financial center where the Yoruba, Igbo, Hausa, and many others live together and consider themselves Nigerians above all. The wounds left by the Civil War will remain. The past will not be forgotten. But the new generation of Nigerians, part of a very young population that has not lived through those dark years, wants to look toward the future, to move on as a united nation. The adoption of better policies (a better environment for business, a less bloated public sector, the enforcement of the rule of law, a serious crackdown on red tape and corruption, and a more efficient management of natural resources), similar to what Botswana has achieved, would convince some of the many highly educated Nigerians living abroad to return and contribute further to the growth of their nation. We are convinced that if the right policies were enacted, southern Nigeria (especially the southeast) would emerge as one of the fastest growing economies in the world.

Chapter 8

United States

F ew books have better portrayed the human consequences of the 2008 financial crisis on American communities than *Janesville*, written by Washington Post journalist Amy Goldstein and published in 2017. A town of 60,000 inhabitants in the state of Wisconsin, Janesville was home to a large General Motors factory, the biggest employer in town until the shutdown of the plant in December 2008, which resulted in more than 1,200 plant workers and as many as 4,500 people in total, including local suppliers, losing their jobs. Many other local businesses were affected to some extent, such as restaurants, bars, and property developers.

Janesville describes the shock and despair that gripped the town. Built in 1910, the plant had been an employer to generations of workers. For most of them, it was more than just work. The close community that was built over the years at their workplace became an important part of their lives, giving them a sense of pride, a feeling of belonging. It is difficult to comprehend the emotions felt by those workers when it was announced that they were being let go. Goldstein followed some of them for several years after the plant closure. Some moved to other towns in search of jobs, commuting back to Janesville over weekends until they retired.

Some tried to learn new skills, often with limited success: Those in their fifties who had never used a computer struggled to find any meaningful work. Some became social workers or prison guards, earning a fraction of what they used to. Half of all retrenched workers had trouble paying for food. Substance abuse and cases of depression surged among the community.[1]

Eventually, things did improve, for Janesville and for the country. The unemployment rate in Janesville, which rose to 14 percent in early 2009, declined over the following years, reaching an all-time low of three percent in 2018 (it rose sharply during the COVID-19 pandemic as it did in the rest of the US, but was down to 3.1 percent by November 2023).[2] Large employers in the state of Wisconsin, such as Harley-Davidson, Kohler, and Manitowoc Cranes, are once again expanding their operations. Since 2017, Taiwanese chip manufacturer Foxconn has invested US$900 million in the state and built a plant thirty miles south of Milwaukee that employs 1,000 workers (although many more were expected).[3] Another example is SHINE Medical Technologies. Founded in 2010, it specializes in medical isotopes and moved its headquarters to Janesville in 2019. The company completed the construction of a new 18,700-square-foot facility in Janesville in mid-2023, producing an isotope that will improve treatments for certain types of cancer.

Janesville represents the industrial heartland of America, which has at times struggled to compete with the likes of Japan and China. Rebounding from the most severe financial crisis in living memory took longer than many had expected, but the economy did rebound strongly. The ongoing pandemic is another case in point: The US economy has bounced back faster and stronger than that of most other nations. America remains one of the main drivers of global growth. This has been made possible by the inherent dynamism of American society: the ability to look forward, to remain confident, and to reinvent itself.

Free and industrious

The United States is the embodiment of free markets (within its national borders). Few other nations rely on market dynamics to provide the most efficient allocation of resources as much as the US. The prices of most goods and services are determined by supply and demand. Few barriers to entry exist in most industries, allowing more competitive firms to replace less competitive ones in a continuous process of creative destruction, making the US one the most productive and innovative nations in the world.

This has been the case throughout America's history. The economic freedom enjoyed by both individuals and companies has historically been much higher compared to Europe, a continent that for centuries had (and, some will argue, still has) a hereditary class structure that prevented social mobility and hindered meritocracy. Large European corporations, with their long and proud history often going back centuries, had little to fear from new competitors, however more productive or innovative they may have been. Alexis de Tocqueville, the French aristocrat who spent nine months touring the US in 1831, considered the restlessness of Americans to be their greatest strength. They would go wherever they saw opportunities, moving from one part of the country to the other, from one industry to another. De Tocqueville met Americans "who have successively been lawyers, farmers, businessmen, ministers of the Gospel, and physicians." As a telling example, while in Connecticut, he found that 36 members of Congress had been born in the state, but only five of them represented it; the others had relocated to other states during their lifetime.[4]

The notion of American freedom is not merely restricted to free markets, but applies to an entire society, one based on democracy and individual liberties. Democracy has been the bedrock of America's political stability, ensuring a smooth transition of power between leaders and preventing the abuse of power. Although a vibrant democracy may not be a requirement for economic freedom and prosperity, it is more conducive to it, facilitating the exchange of ideas that leads to higher innovation and upholding judicial independence for a stronger rule of law.

Free markets do not just work by themselves. They require a robust framework that clearly determines the rules of the game and warrants that those rules are the same for all participants. This requires a stable, independent, clear, and effective US legal system, whether it relates to property and intellectual rights that protect the ownership of assets; bankruptcy laws that ensure an orderly winding down or restructuring of struggling companies; or antitrust laws that protect consumers from predatory business practices such as the abuse of a dominant market position. Intellectual property rights are among the most sophisticated in the world. The state also plays a leading, but often ignored, role in research. Silicon Valley would not have become what it is today without government-sponsored research and government investments in the 1960s and 1970s.

Free markets and democracy have contributed significantly to the rise of America. But the country would not have become the wealthiest nation on the planet without the hard work of its population. The Protestant work ethic prevalent in northern Europe, where most Americans historically came from, focused on hard work, thrift, individual responsibility, integrity, self-reliance, and honesty, shaping American society since its independence. De Tocqueville considered the constant desire to work hard and accumulate wealth as the reason for America's restlessness. School textbooks inculcated children with the virtues of work and thrift. Thrift education provided guidance to students on how to manage their finances and plan for the future and formed part of the common curriculum until the early twentieth century.[5] Freed from rigid social structures in Europe, such as the right of the first-born child to inherit the parent's entire estate or the difficulty of acquiring and selling properties, Americans had a greater opportunity to accumulate wealth if they worked toward that goal. This became known as the American dream, the idea that everyone can make it as long as they work hard. Many successful Americans hailed from modest backgrounds. Andrew Carnegie (founder of Carnegie Steel), Henry Miller (who built a cattle empire in the late nineteenth century), Samuel Walton (founder of Walmart), and many others started dirt poor, but were given the opportunity to succeed, an opportunity that would not have been made available to them in most other countries at that time. In America, much more so than in Europe, few were guaranteed wealth; they had to earn it.

It is this combination of an industrious population and a free society where that industriousness could be rewarded, or where a lack of industriousness would be punished more so than in nations where many could rely on their privileges of birth, that explains the formidable rise of the country — a rise threatened today by an erosion of values and the emergence of new competitors.

Less and less equal

There is another side to the Janesville story. The closure of the General Motors (GM) plant had its origins in the financial crisis, but there was a larger factor at play: globalization. Since the late 1970s, US manufacturers have faced increasing competition from countries producing cheaper or higher-quality goods (or both). This was also a time when the country embraced free trade agreements, giving an incentive to US manufacturers to relocate large parts of their production abroad. GM's Janesville factory employed 7,000 workers in 1970; only 1,200 workers remained at the time of its closure in 2008.[6] The workers of Janesville did eventually find new jobs, but a vast majority of those jobs paid far less and often required fewer skills. Janesville illustrates the damage that globalization has wrecked on low- or middle-class American workers. On average, low-income Americans have not seen any increase in their wages for the past 30 years (adjusted for inflation). The richest Americans have, however, become much richer, increasing inequalities to levels last seen during the roaring 1920s. Higher inequalities have generated among the less affluent a sense of unfairness, frustration, anger, and, in some cases, a feeling of hopelessness at times leading to social unrest. Between 1980 and 2010, life expectancy for the poorest 20 percent of Americans declined, but continued to rise for the wealthiest 20 percent.[7]

Low unemployment rates mean that few people are actively looking for a job, either because they already have one or because they have stopped looking for one. But for those workers who have a job, employment and unemployment figures do not tell us anything about the *quality* of those jobs. There is a growing divide between a shrinking number of very highly skilled jobs and a growing number of jobs that are low-skilled, low-paid, and offer little protection. Many of those employed in the gig economy have little hope of improving their skills or their wages. One study found that American workers who lost their job as a result of increased trade with China and have had to join another industry lost on average 20 percent of their income.[8] The Job Quality Index (JQI), which compares the number of "high-quality" jobs, defined as those that pay higher than the average income, to "low-quality" jobs that pay below the average income, has gradually declined over the years.[9] Jobs are available, but *good* jobs are becoming a rarity.

Economists will argue that globalization is good for a country *as a whole*, reducing the cost of goods and services and providing opportunities for local companies to expand their operations abroad. This is probably true, but it is of little consolation to those stuck in a low-paying job with little hope of advancement. International trade may be beneficial overall, but the distribution of those benefits has been uneven. Those distributional aspects of globalization have for too long been ignored. US companies have mostly gained from globalization, but a large number of workers, especially those living and working in areas that have been the most negatively affected by globalization, have suffered from it. Even the overall gains of free trade for a country with a large and strong domestic market may not be as significant as commonly thought.[10]

The rise in inequalities has coincided with a steep decline in social trust. In the 1970s, about 40–45 percent of Americans felt that most people could be trusted. But since the mid-1980s, that proportion has gradually declined, and today less than a third of Americans trust others.[11] Fewer Americans participate in civic organizations.[12]

The 1980s and 1990s profoundly changed American society for several reasons. Migration from countries with lower social trust has reduced overall trust in the US. Social trust may be further reduced (but also occasionally increased) depending on how migrants interact with the rest of society. This should not be interpreted as a criticism of migration. Migration provides several economic, social, and cultural benefits to society. As a new generation of migrants integrates into society, the long-term benefits generally outweigh the short-term challenges. America has prospered in part because of successive waves of migrants, who over time have fully settled into their new country and contributed to its growth.

But it is not just migration that can explain the loss of social trust in the US. Corporate America in the 1980s underwent significant shifts. The rise of financialization, the focus on shareholder value, and the predatory corporate tactics employed by some during that era destabilized traditional US companies. The income of CEOs and fund managers at times reached staggering levels, with little justification for it. An increasing disconnect between those at the top of the corporate ladder and workers down the chain has led to the latter losing trust in the system and the former having few qualms about relocating production outside the US, even if that meant the loss of jobs back home. The trend continued in the 1990s with the rise of China and the signing of free trade agreements, including the North American Free Trade Agreement (NAFTA) in 1994, which generated a wave of delocalizations to Mexico. In the 2000s, faster Internet connections and broader network access enabled US companies to offshore or outsource services to the likes of India and the Philippines: customer service, accounting, and various other functions. US workers could not compete on costs: An Indian worker earns a fraction of what the US worker makes. But US workers are also finding it increasingly difficult to compete on skills: Indian workers have become increasingly well-educated and are willing to put in very long hours, working nightshifts to adapt to US time zones if needed. It is not only trust in others that has declined but also the trust that Americans have in their institutions. Whereas more than two-thirds of Americans trusted their government in the 1960s, less than a fifth of them still do.[13] Without trust, democratic institutions are losing their legitimacy in an increasingly polarized nation.

This trend has not taken place in other developed countries as much as it has in the US, with the notable exception of the UK, which went through a very similar process of financialization and high pay for top managers in the 1980s and 1990s. Few European, Japanese, or Australian companies have offshored their services to India or relocalized production for domestic sales to lower-cost countries. Social trust in most of those countries has remained at levels similar to the 1970s. Inequalities have increased, but far less than in the US or the UK. Some will argue that this is because taxes and redistributions are higher in those countries compared to the US, but even *pre-tax* income inequalities in those countries have not increased much.[14] The different outcomes seen in those countries also gives less credence to another common explanation for rising inequalities: accelerating technological change, hurting lower-skilled workers the most. Technological disruption is likely to increase inequalities, but perhaps not as much as we may believe, since it fails to explain why Europe, Japan, and Australia, which have all been exposed to the same technological changes as the US or the UK, have remained more equal societies.

In those countries, higher social trust has contributed to a stronger social fabric, preventing inequalities from widening as much as they did in the US or the UK. CEOs are paid much less than their US counterparts, with little impact on their actual performance. Those countries have kept a stronger sense of community, of togetherness, maintaining healthier relations with various stakeholders, not just shareholders. The CEO of a German company is likely to think twice before laying off a large chunk of her employees to set up a factory in China or a call center in India. That is not to say that large German or Japanese manufacturers will not expand their operations outside their borders, but this usually caters to markets outside their home country. US companies that have embraced globalization have become more efficient, probably more so than companies elsewhere that have been less willing to relocate production or services abroad. Some had no choice: If their competitors lower their operating costs, they have to follow suit to remain competitive. But this has come at the cost of a more fractured American society.

Possible remedies

How can inequalities be reduced?

Let us start with what does not work. Social trust is very unlikely to rise again, at least not in the near future. Efforts to reverse the gradual decline of social trust will not succeed. Changing the economic model from free markets to one where competition and price-setting are determined by the state is a recipe for disaster. Regulating the pay of CEOs and fund managers has never been implemented, for good reason:

Figuring out the appropriate level of pay for top managers is best left to the markets. It is for shareholders and other investors to defend their interests. At best, policies could be put in place to improve the incentive and ability of those market participants to exercise greater control over excessive pay.

Then, there is the universal basic income or UBI. With automation, artificial intelligence, and other technological change, there is increasing fear that robots will be taking over our jobs. Record low unemployment tells us that we remain very far from such a scenario becoming a reality. A UBI that covers basic expenses may work, providing better financial security to those who need it most without reducing the incentive to work hard. But a UBI high enough that it covers most expenses and replaces the income generated from work would be a very dangerous experiment, one which is bound to fail as it will significantly reduce the incentive to work, especially in a country with declining trust. In April 2021, there were a record 9.3 million vacancies with 4 million workers, another record, quitting their job during that month; for those receiving higher unemployment benefits than what they were earning at their previous job, there is little incentive to get back to work.[15] An exception could be displaced workers above a certain age who may struggle to find another job and for whom a guaranteed income could make more sense.

With that in mind, we can think of four possible solutions when it comes to reducing inequalities in the US.

The first is to improve the "employability" of workers, that is, their ability to move into jobs with better prospects. This is about retraining workers, equipping them with better skills. The US provides training (as well as cash handouts) to those who lost their jobs because of international trade under the Trade Adjustment Assistance (TAA). The results so far have been mixed, partly because the program has not been scaled up.[16] It is difficult to learn new skills, especially for older workers, but there are few alternatives in a world of increasing technological change. The employability of workers can also improve when they relocate to places that offer better opportunities. Yet Americans are much less willing than their ancestors to move to different locations, mainly because they do not wish to venture into the unknown and leave behind an environment that they are familiar with.

The second option is to better distribute the benefits of globalization. This typically involves increasing taxes and social welfare. It will not reduce *pre-tax* inequalities and it will not give laid-off workers their job back, but it should at least reduce *post-tax* inequalities. When it comes to taxes, and more specifically personal taxes, discussions have been mainly about the top (or marginal) income tax rate. This is a mistake. As an extreme example, a top rate of 90 percent that applies to those earning more than one hundred million dollars a year will make no difference. What really matters is the overall structure of the tax rates (the rates that apply to each income threshold), the type of taxes levied (such as the gap between capital gains and income tax rates), and closing tax loopholes, of which many exist.

Tax revenues in the US represent 24 percent of the GDP, much lower than the average 34 percent for OECD countries.[17] Tax rates, for both individuals and companies, should, however, not be excessive. Those who advocate for top income tax rates of 50 percent or more, pointing out that the top tax rate during much of the 1950s was 91 percent, should realize that the top rate in the 1950s only applied to a very small portion of *additional* income declared by a very small portion of taxpayers and that tax rules back then were riddled with loopholes.[18] Tax revenues in the 1950s were no higher than they are now (nor at any time after WWII).[19] Therefore, increasing the top tax rate for the wealthiest of Americans is very unlikely to generate more tax revenues. This can only work in countries with high levels of social and political trust, such as Nordic nations where governments have a much higher legitimacy in collecting taxes and distributing benefits. Rich Americans will not sit idle if they feel that their *effective* tax rate (the total taxes they pay compared to their income) becomes excessive. We are not suggesting that they will work less, but they will find ways to lower their tax bill, whether that involves registering companies in tax-friendly Delaware or other offshore jurisdictions or even renouncing their citizenship. Companies with an excessive tax burden may renounce investments into projects that would otherwise have been viable. The effective tax rate of wealthy American citizens and corporations should be increased, but within reasonable limits.

Higher taxes and redistributions are not an attack on free markets. People often have an ideological view of such matters. But as Nordic countries have shown, it is very much possible for companies and individuals to operate in an environment of free and fair competition with limited state intervention, and for the state to nevertheless play a major role in redistributing wealth. Higher taxes, as long as they do not become excessive, are unlikely to reduce economic growth.

The third option is tariffs. For tariffs to be effective, they need to cover multiple origins, otherwise they can easily be circumvented. When the US imposed tariffs on Chinese tires in 2009, total tire imports into the US actually *rose*, as other countries filled in the void left by Chinese exporters. Well-calibrated tariffs could make goods produced in the US more competitive, sheltered from foreign competition from lower-cost countries. They are, however, unlikely to result in US companies relocating factories back to the US. There is little evidence of that following the tariffs implemented under the Trump administration, with US companies seemingly adopting a wait-and-see approach. Tariffs also have drawbacks. Other countries will retaliate, hurting American businesses that rely on exports. Tariffs are mostly imposed on goods, less so on services. Services represent more than 75 percent of GDP, 80 percent of all US employment, and contribute the most to GDP growth.[20] This reduces the overall impact of tariffs, although the impact will be larger in US states with a large manufacturing sector.

The fourth option would be to force US companies to manufacture at home products that are sold in the country and, in the case of services, to handle all operations for the US market within the country. A US car manufacturer selling cars in the US would have to produce them within the country. All functions that relate to sales within the US would similarly have to be conducted domestically. This is admittedly a drastic measure, one that would reduce the profitability of US companies and increase prices for goods and services. If Apple was forced to domestically manufacture IPhones sold in the US, IPhones would be more expensive, hurting US consumers. But it would also create better jobs and possibly higher standards of living for the US middle class. A softer version of such an approach is to provide incentives for US companies to return production and processes to the US, such as subsidies, tax breaks, or other legal incentives. One such example is the Inflation Reduction Act which provides tax breaks for the purchase of electric vehicles and has incentivized car manufacturers to move production to the US.

An erosion of values?

Has America lost its traditional values? Some Americans believe so and see their society in decline. 77 percent of Americans are fairly or very worried about their nation's values. Most believe that, in the future, the country will be less important in the world, more politically divided, and the economy will be weaker.[21]

We have seen how social trust declined over time. What about thrift and hard work? Has "play and spend" replaced "work and save"? Thrift certainly seems to have eroded. Personal savings rates have declined, from 15 percent in the nineteenth century to 10 percent in the 1970s to 5 percent by 2020 (the pandemic did result in a spike in savings as many people were reluctantly saving more during lockdowns but have since resumed their usual spending habits after restrictions were lifted).[22] Higher consumption and debt in the US have coincided with the rise of consumerism. Credit has become cheaper and much more readily available. Few are now willing to wait years of saving to acquire a car or the latest smartphone. Two centuries ago, de Tocqueville presciently worried that the US might develop so great a "taste for physical gratification" that citizens would be "carried away, and lose all self-restraint."[23] The 1980s witnessed an explosion of debt that carried on for several decades. Homeowners could realize their dream of acquiring a property, as mortgages became more readily available and regulations were eased. Corporations piled up on bonds and other forms of corporate debt to expand their operations, either organically or through acquisitions. Banks played a key role in providing the debt that Americans so desperately wanted. Those banks are now much more regulated, but the need of Americans to incur debt has not changed and is unlikely to change any time soon.

As for hard work, since we are unable to properly measure it, it is very difficult to assess whether Americans are less hardworking than their ancestors. Some will argue that television, video games, social media, and other forms of entertainment have turned generations away from hard work and toward more affluence and hedonism. Maybe. But we think the main shift when it comes to the notion of hard work has taken place outside US borders, not within them.

American Factory, an Oscar-winning documentary produced in 2017, tells the story of Fuyao, a large Chinese automotive glassmaker that acquired a plant in Ohio in 2010, hiring around 2,300 workers, including 200 from China. As the plant started operating, there was a lot of excitement and hope. Most of the American workers were middle-class, middle-age Ohioans whose livelihoods had been deeply affected by the financial crisis. Many used to work for General Motors at a nearby plant until it was shut down. At Fuyao, they earned only a fraction of what they used to make, but at least they had a job. Over time, relations with Chinese workers became increasingly tense. The plant started to lose money and most of the American managers were replaced by Chinese ones. Some of the American workers pushed for a union to defend their rights. Each side tended to work on its own, rarely interacting with the other, making is a rather dysfunctional organization.

At the heart of the issue is hard work and what it means to be working hard. For the Chinese, the Americans did not work hard enough. They were too slow in performing their tasks, unwilling to work overtime or on weekends, and taking too many holidays. But hard work is a relative concept. The American workers were convinced that they worked hard. Some of them were invited to Fuyao's headquarters in China. They realized then how much more hardworking the Chinese were, with those who had migrated from their villages returning home only once or twice a year to see their families.

The American workers at Fuyao saw things very differently. They felt exploited by the Chinese. They used to earn $28 an hour at GM; that went down to $12 an hour at Fuyao (it later increased to $14 a few days before workers were asked to vote to join a union). How can one make a decent living from that? Not only did the Chinese want them to work excruciatingly long hours, they put them under a lot of stress and were somewhat careless about safety conditions. One worker, who got injured at the plant a few months after joining Fuyao, claimed not to have had a single work-related injury when working for GM.

Working conditions in China, Vietnam, and India are considered exploitative by western standards. The forefathers of US workers had fought for better work conditions. Decades of social progress in the US should not be sacrificed. But there is an urgent need to move toward more value-adding industries and for manufacturing workers to upgrade their skills. If American workers cannot compete on price, they must compete on quality, similar to what many German or Swiss manufacturers have done. A forklift operator in his early thirties who believes he can simply do the exact same job for the next 30 years before retirement is mistaken. Workers with such a mindset will struggle.

Some values in the US may be eroded, but at a much slower pace than what is sometimes believed. People tend to have a nostalgic view of the past, convinced that things were so much better back then. But the US remains a formidable nation. It continues to grow faster than many other nations at a similar stage of development. It will remain one of the most innovative countries, attracting many of the brightest minds from around the world. Rising inequalities are clearly an issue that needs to be addressed, but to put things into perspective, China has become almost as unequal as the US as measured by its GINI coefficient.[24] Yet, few people talk about inequalities in China as dramatically as they do in the US, probably because China's rise is much more recent and improvements in living standards from one generation to the other were evident. Yet China too will at some point face the same challenges that higher inequalities generate.

There is no reason why the US cannot reinvent itself again, as it has done throughout its history. In this chapter, we have focused quite heavily on declining US industries and regions, but many others are thriving and will continue to do so. The country has become more polarized, between different political affiliations, ethnic groups, and social classes. But its biggest strength is its ability to come together as a nation at times when it is most needed. The displaced workers in Janesville came together as a community, helping each other out. It is during difficult times that people show their true values and move forward in search of a brighter collective future.

Chapter 9

Greece

By 2015, Stavros Hatzakos had become increasingly disillusioned each time he gazed through the windows of his office. As the general manager of Terminal 1 of the port of Piraeus, Greece's largest port located in the suburbs of Athens, he could see a stark contrast: Terminal 1 was almost empty, with hardly a container in sight. Just a few hundred yards away, Terminals 2 and 3 were bustling with activity with an incessant flow of vessels loading and unloading their containers. Terminals 2 and 3 had been managed over the past 6 years by Cosco, one of China's largest state-owned container operators.

Back in 2009, as Greece experienced a severe recession and was forced to sell some of its public assets, Cosco acquired a 35-year concession to operate about half of the Piraeus port's capacity for US$650 million, seeing the port as a gateway to Europe for Chinese exports. Following that acquisition, the Chinese-operated section of Piraeus port became one of the fastest-growing container ports in the world. By 2015, only one container line was still splitting its activity between the Greek-administered part of the port and the one managed by Cosco; all other container lines had permanently switched to Terminals 2 and 3.[1] A year later, Cosco took control of the entire port, including its passenger ferry services, and pledged over US$500 million in additional investments. In 2021, it increased its stake from 51 percent to 67 percent.

To understand why container shipping companies were much keener to work with Cosco than with the previous Greek-led management, we need to go back to the days before Cosco. In 2008, a port worker was paid on average US$50,000 a year, with some paid as high as US$180,000 annually, fifteen times the official average wage in Greece.[2] Crane operators, who could operate cranes for no more than four consecutive hours for safety reasons as per EU regulations, would leave work for the day after completing their shift, but still be paid their full salaries. Nine workers were required to operate a gantry crane. Despite those rather generous work conditions, the port was marred by frequent strikes as workers continuously pushed for better conditions. Loading and unloading rates were among the lowest in Europe compared to other container ports. Container lines also complained of being asked by port officials for additional "fees" if they wanted their vessels to be prioritized over others.

Cosco's arrival felt like a cultural shock. Higher productivity would be achieved through hard work. In the colorful words of Fu Cheng Qiu, who managed the port operations for Cosco, "If you want a higher salary you first need to work hard. Not lie on the beach and drink beer. Learn from the Germans! Work hard, never be lazy and always work seriously. Hard work — happy life."[3] Operating a gantry crane now requires four workers instead of nine. This did not decrease loading and unloading rates; on the contrary, turnaround times at Terminals 2 and 3 became twice as fast as those at the Greek-managed Terminal 1. Crane operators, after their 4-hour shift of moving containers, work an additional four hours on the docks. The number of departments has been cut in half. Cosco also invested in modernizing port facilities and equipment. The crane system was upgraded, deep-water docks were installed to accommodate the latest generation of giant container ships, a new oil terminal was completed, and transit capacity between the port and inland railway networks was improved. The company reached out to multinationals such as Hewlett-Packard to promote the use of Piraeus as a distribution center for their operations in Europe. In the end, the annual fee that Cosco paid to Terminal 1 as part of the acquisition agreement with the Greek government was higher than the entire annual revenue generated by Terminal 1 through its own freight activity.

This transformation has not been without its critics. Cosco is accused of benefiting from Greece's woes at the expense of its workers, importing Chinese working standards. Few Chinese workers have been hired, but wages have been slashed: Workers earn about a third of what they used to. Most employees are hired on a temporary basis through local agencies and given little protection by unions. Greek port workers are understandably unhappy about this turn of events. They used to enjoy better pay and shorter working hours. Some have agreed to join Cosco, but others have left, unwilling to adapt to this new reality. The problem with the old model is that it had become unsustainable. The country was living above its means; sooner or later, things would come to a halt.

What went wrong?

Back in 2001, as Greece was preparing to join the Eurozone, it had already accumulated a lot of debt. With a public debt-to-GDP ratio above 100 percent, the debt owed by the Greek government was higher than what the country was producing in a year. Greek politicians were not overly worried by this: They saw vast amounts of money from abroad pouring into the country. French, Dutch, and German banks were lured by Greece's growth potential and invested heavily in Greek bonds, banks, and other industries. Not only was the money plentiful, it was also cheap: Interest rates on 10-year Greek bonds were only slightly higher than German bonds, at around 5 percent.

Over the next 7 years, Greece continued to borrow. What it borrowed, it spent, with government expenditures growing much faster than revenues. This led to budget deficits that started to swell, reaching 13 percent of GDP by 2008. In other words, the Greek government was spending so much that the public deficit in 2008 represented 13 percent of everything the country produced during that year. Those were the official figures, which would later turn out to be unreliable as Greece had been rather creative in its accounting, exploiting loopholes in EU regulations and going as far as pledging future landing fees at its airports, highway tolls, and lottery gains as part of a scheme to cook its numbers. Higher deficits were financed by ever-higher levels of debt. Yet the accumulation of debt and deficits raised few eyebrows in Athens. Greece was now part of the Eurozone and keen to expand its economy further.

By 2008, with the global financial crisis in full swing, investors scrambled to repatriate overseas investments. As international appetite for foreign debt faded, the cost of servicing that debt went up. In Greece, problems were exacerbated by the fact that the country had been dishonest with its official figures. Debt and deficit levels were much worse than expected. By now, very concerned by the state of Greece's finances, foreign investors demanded much higher returns on public debt: from 5 percent in 2009 to 9 percent in 2010, 16 percent in 2011, and 22 percent in 2012. Before the crisis hit, Greece had relied on new foreign investment to service its mounting debt. But as investors pulled out, the country found itself unable to repay its debt. Greece essentially ran out of cash.

This short description of what happened to Greece's economy does not go down to the root of the problem: Why did Greece borrow so much? Why did the likes of Germany not borrow as much and how did they manage to avoid finding themselves in a similar predicament? Our focus here is not so much on the aftermath of the crisis. Greece was forced into a series of painful reforms by its international creditors. Whether things would have turned out differently if less austerity had been imposed on Greece and its people and whether Greece should have more seriously considered pulling out of the Eurozone to allow its currency to depreciate are questions that will continue to be debated for many years. What we are focused on here is why Greece got into this mess in the first place. It did not get into this mess by being an innocent victim of the greediness of international creditors. It got into this mess by seriously mismanaging its economy.

Too few revenues

A deep fiscal deficit can be caused by two things: not enough revenues or too much spending. Greece suffered from both. Widespread abuse of state money over the years and an overly generous pension system are largely to blame. This fiscal profligacy that began in the 1980s was adopted by governments across the political spectrum who, in the words of journalist and author Yannis Palaiologos, "offered its [citizens] the same seductive diet of lifetime government jobs, immunity from the taxman, a steady stream of public contracts and fat pensions just as their hair began to turn grey."[4]

No one knows the true number, but Greeks are believed to have evaded 10–30 billion euros of taxes every year.[5] That compares to annual tax revenues of about 70 billion euros, so a substantial amount of revenues failed to end up in public coffers. In the years leading up to the crisis (2000–2007), the economy grew significantly, and so did wages. But tax revenues did not increase as much.[6] This is unusual: One would expect that those who earn more would pay more taxes, especially for a country with a progressive income tax system. But in Greece, people were finding all sorts of ways to evade taxes, taking advantage of a complex system that saw virtually no enforcement by local authorities. Since 1975, Greece enacted 250 tax laws and 115,000 tax-related ministerial decisions.[7] No one knew anymore what was legally permissible, and no one really cared.

Tax evasion seems embedded in the social fabric of the country: Most Greeks would know of fellow citizens who at one point or another evaded taxes. 35 percent of Greek citizens would readily evade their taxes if the opportunity arose, because "everyone does it."[8] The biggest culprits are independent workers, of which Greece has twice as many compared to most other EU countries. In 2011, two-thirds of all self-employed Greeks declared an annual income below the tax-free limit of 12,000 euros. During that same year, half of all taxpayers, about 2.8 million citizens, each paid an average of just 21 euros of income taxes.[9] It is rather difficult to plug a growing fiscal deficit when half of your working population pays 21 euros of annual taxes.

Tax evasion occurs at every income level, but the state loses out the most with its wealthiest independent workers, those who have access to ingenious schemes and the ability to hide their cash in foreign bank accounts. No one really knows how much is deposited in those offshore accounts, but the number is probably in the tens of billions of euros. A typical scheme could be an architect who renovates a house for 100,000 euros. He invoices his client for 20,000 euros and asks for 75,000 euros to be transferred to his private account in Switzerland (giving a 5-percent discount to his client for agreeing to the scheme). This allows him to significantly reduce income and value-added taxes. Doctors, lawyers, financial advisers, and many other self-employed workers have similarly abused the system over the years. This type of behavior is certainly not specific to Greece; it occurs to some extent in every country. But in Greece, tax evasion reached epic proportions.

Too much spending

If the state earned too little, it also spent too much. Public expenditures as a proportion of the GDP were much higher than in the rest of Europe. Greece was spending more on its military as a percentage of the GDP than any other European country. Public workers were being paid more than their counterparts in the private sector and seeing high wage increases each year, in most cases unrelated to their actual performance.[10] The island of Zakynthos became infamous for having 700 blind residents, nine times the average rate of blindness in the EU, some of whom were registered as taxi or truck drivers. An agency that was formed in 1957 to supervise the draining of a lake which disappeared that same year was still employing 30 public workers 50 years later. Doctors have been known to perform cosmetic surgeries and declare them as appendectomies, which were covered by medical insurance.[11] Those examples are not mere anecdotes that the international press loves to report on; they are symptomatic of the inefficiencies and the lack of accountability in the way public finances were managed, or more appropriately, mismanaged.

While the abuse of disability, unemployment, and medical benefits is clearly a concern, their impact on Greece's finances remained limited. Spending in those areas in the years leading to the crisis was fairly modest by international comparison and on par with other EU countries. A greater concern relates to pensions. The Greek population is aging rapidly, as it is in most developed countries; but, in Greece, the problem is compounded by an overly generous and unmonitored pension system.

Officially, people retire at 61 years on average, but in reality, most public workers retire in their early fifties in a country with a life expectancy of 80 years old. No country in the EU spends as much for its pensions as Greece does, with annual pension costs representing about 20 percent of GDP.[12] The Greek pensions system was ranked as the least sustainable among 50 countries in 2011.[13] A quarter of the population is retired and most of them earn almost as much as they did when they were working. Here as well, there was plenty of abuse. Some people were still receiving their pensions long after they died because news of their death had not been communicated to the state department administering pensions. Their family members happily continued to cash in the monthly allowances. In the past, people relied heavily on family ties for support.

That support has been gradually replaced by the state. The crisis has further complicated matters as people may have the willingness but not the ability to support family members as their own savings have dwindled over the years.

The issue is not so much the level of pensions distributed to retirees. Those amounts are relatively low, at times below the official poverty line. Reducing them will have little impact on Greece's finances, and reducing the pensions of those retirees who have to make do with a few hundred euros a month, as international creditors have demanded, is morally questionable. The real problem when it comes to Greek pensions is that too many people are retiring too early with too few active workers financially supporting them. For every retired Greek, there are just three active workers, the lowest ratio in Europe after Italy.[14] Another reason why Greece has so few active workers is that, with a large informal sector believed to account for 25–30 percent of the economy, many do hold a job but do not declare it. They avoid paying income taxes and making social contributions but still receive unemployment benefits. Even when the economy was booming, the unemployment rate remained higher than the EU average. But when the crisis hit and the economy began to shrink by a quarter each year, unemployment surged. A massive 60 percent of those between 15 years and 24 years of age were officially without a job as both the public and private sectors were forced to drastically reduce their workforce.[15]

Students unable to find a job after graduating extended their studies or simply left the country for greener pastures. 120,000 students are believed to have migrated in the first 2 years that followed the start of the crisis, many of them highly qualified.[16] As a result, Greece ended up in a situation where it financed the education of its most skilled students for two decades and once they were fully trained and able to contribute to the economy, they left — another tragedy in a country that had already experienced many.

It was not only the state that spent too much. Greece has never been a nation of savers. Its gross savings rate has oscillated around 15 percent of the GDP since the early 1990s. During the boom years of 2005–2008, it gradually went down, below 10 percent, half of what the EU saves on average. Hardly anyone was saving, whether citizens, businesses, or the government. People received a higher income, but never bothered to save much of it for a rainy day. Such low rates of saving would prove unsustainable. In the absence of domestic savings, the few meaningful investments made by the country had to be financed through foreign borrowing.

Lack of trust

We have so far described the factors that led to the crisis, but we have not gone to the roots of it. Why was there so much more abuse of public money in Greece than elsewhere?

The widespread abuse of Greece's institutions has its roots in a lack of social trust. Only 18 percent of Greeks believe that others can generally be trusted, one of the lowest proportions among EU countries.[17] One would have expected social trust to decline even more with the crisis. It did not: it remained stable or even increased slightly. That is because the crisis was not perceived in Greece as an internal conflict, but as a national "fight" against international creditors. People felt they were all in the same boat. An "us against them" mentality emerged which united people. Iceland experienced a similar rise in social trust as its economy was disintegrating.[18] Then again, social trust has remained low in Greece. Political trust is also very low with just one in ten Greeks trusting their political institutions, a result that should come as no surprise given the economic situation of the country back then.[19]

Having generous subsidies in a low-trust country without adequate controls in place is a recipe for disaster. People will abuse the system if they can get away with it. And in Greece, there were no controls. The few that did get caught received minimal punishment, which gave them a renewed incentive to continue abusing the system. A simple example of how the lack of controls in a low-trust society leads to chaos is the Athens metro system. The network had no turnstiles to access the platforms and few inspectors. Instead, it relied on trust: Trusting that its commuters would pay for their ticket. That could not work in a country with little trust: Very few commuters actually paid for a ticket and the operator of the metro ended up with losses worth tens of millions of euros each year. The absence of controllers and security cameras also meant that pickpockets operated freely, often targeting tourists. The national train system fared no better: few controls, nominal fines, and millions of euros of losses. Greece is unsurprisingly one of the most unequal countries in Europe.[20] As one would expect from a nation with little social trust, most taxes collected are not income taxes but indirect taxes, such as VAT, fuel and tobacco taxes, affecting the poor more than the rich (as a proportion of their income).

Elusive change

Abuses of the system can only stop with effective controls and penalties for those that break the rules. Such measures are sorely lacking. Hardly anyone gets caught evading taxes, abusing social benefits, or accepting bribes. Businesses routinely complain of having to pay bribes to fast-track applications for various permits. Setting up a new business takes years.

What about the very few who do get caught? In most cases, they are simply asked to repay what they earned illicitly and often given the option to do so in installments — a good incentive to pursue their fraudulent activities. In 2010, Greece was given a golden opportunity to go after its wealthiest tax evaders when its government was handed over a list containing the names of almost 2,000 Greek citizens with undeclared bank accounts in Switzerland (the "Lagarde List"). The list was sent to local tax authorities, who never acted on it. The finance minister who initially received the list allegedly erased three names from it, all relatives of his. His successor claimed to have lost the list; it is only when another copy of the list was requested from abroad that he remembered the list to be in his secretary's drawer. By 2012, still no action had been taken. That year, a reporter published the names of those appearing in the list in a magazine. Displaying unusual haste, the authorities arrested him the very next day for breaching privacy laws (he was later found not guilty).

Even when alleged fraudsters are brought to justice, they have little to fear. The Greek justice system is overly complicated, slow, and arguably corrupt. Court proceedings for serious tax cases can take up to 10 years. Enforcing contracts is nearly three times more time-consuming on average compared to other OECD countries.[21] According to Transparency International, the entire judicial system suffers from a "mentality of tolerance and fatalism with regard to corruption [that] supports petty corruption and perpetuates the bottlenecks in institutions which stand strongly against any reform."[22] Greece needs to impose punishments that act as a deterrent for people not to engage in such practices. Heavy fines should be meted out and extended jail terms imposed for the more serious crimes so that people think twice before evading taxes or taking a bribe. Public servants found guilty of taking bribes should be dismissed from their job and face severe penalties. The activities of independent workers require much better monitoring: If the assets they own cannot be justified by their declared revenues, they need to be prosecuted and those assets confiscated. Increasing tax revenues in Greece should not necessarily be about increasing tax rates, it should be about enforcing and simplifying existing tax regulations.

The public sector, which employs a quarter of Greek workers, provides no incentive to work hard. Whether they perform well or not, workers will receive the same income and their jobs are protected for life. The public sector needs a complete overhaul. Hiring must be done on merit and not because of connections as is too often the case. One way to do this is through anonymous resumes and the involvement of multiple hiring decision-makers. Those who do not perform should be given warnings and, if their performance does not improve, they should be dismissed. Those who do perform need to be rewarded, through monetary compensation and promotions. When it comes to pensions, the retirement age must be raised and early retirement seriously curtailed. The official retirement age is irrelevant if no one is actually affected by it. Early retirement should be the exception rather than the norm. If controls cannot be put in place or if they remain ineffective, then the size of the state needs to be reduced. There is simply no other choice. More industries should be privatized (but in an orderly fashion, not at fire-sale prices). Most sectors where the state enjoys a monopolistic position should be opened to private competitors.

Domestic markets need to become more competitive. Greece ranks 79th in the world for ease of doing business, similar to Mongolia and Zambia.[23] New businesses must be allowed to be set up and operate on an equal footing with more established companies, in a free and fair environment, one that upholds the rule of law. If those changes can be put in place, Greece's brightest students will have a better incentive to remain in the country and those who have left may consider returning.

A (slightly) brighter future

The Greek population has gone through a decade of tremendous hardship. For an economy to lose a quarter of its income each year for several years is almost unheard of. GDP fell much more and the depression went on for much longer than what most observers had predicted. A crisis of such proportions for a developed country was last seen during the Great Depression of the 1930s in the US.

It was a classic boom-and-bust scenario in which an economy over-heats, and a bubble forms. Spending became the mantra across the country. Banks lent freely. People and businesses, blinded by their euphoric state, failed to realize that at some point the music would stop as growth became unsustainable. Contrary to many bubbles where the excesses are generated by the private sector, in Greece, the state also participated in the binge, spending wildly and ending bankrupt. During such periods of "irrational exuberance," the only voice of reason is often the central bank that can, according to a former Federal Reserve Chairman, "take away the punch bowl just when the party gets started."[24] But having joined the Eurozone, Greece no longer had the ability to adjust domestic interest rates or depreciate its currency.

The measures imposed by international creditors, which included brutal austerity at times targeting the most vulnerable sections of the population, are highly questionable. Greece today sits on a mountain of debt that, in all likelihood, it will never be able to repay. But the wide-spread belief held in Greece that the country is an innocent victim of foreign greed and that the only reason why the economy spiraled out of control is because of its international creditors is clearly mistaken. If things are going to change in Greece, that perception, too, needs to change.

Things have certainly improved since those dark years. They had to: At some point, the memory of past events becomes more distant, even though the crisis itself will never be forgotten by those who experienced it. People and businesses have become less pessimistic about the country's future. As of December 2023, the country was growing at twice the Eurozone average and its public debt had been upgraded to investment grade. Unemployment is the lowest in a decade. Some foreign debt is being repaid early. Greece was not spared by COVID-19, which dealt a heavy blow to its economy, but it recovered well. A higher retirement age of 67 years has been introduced. Fewer cases of corruption have been reported by Transparency International. Some Greeks living abroad are cautiously coming back. Turnstiles have finally been installed at some stations of the Athens metro.

And, yet, one cannot help but cast a suspicious glance at the real effectiveness of those measures. The official retirement age may have been increased to 67, but hardly anyone retires at that age: It will take at least a generation for that to happen. A tax armistice yielded disappointing results: Many Greeks continue to under-declare their revenues and hide their money in offshore bank accounts. Public workers who were dismissed were almost all temporary workers; the permanent ones still have a job for life. Some commuters hop over the turnstiles of the Athens metro in the absence of monitoring by inspectors or cameras.

Greece had no choice but to implement most of these measures and did so half-heartedly. What was most needed, stricter controls and penalties for offenders, is still lacking. While the worst abuses of public funds have abated and Greece should not find itself in another major financial crisis anytime soon, its economy is unlikely to grow strongly for an extended period of time. Corruption and inefficiencies will remain a drag on the economy. The port of Piraeus, with its long and proud history going back to the 5th century BC when Athens fortified it to defend the city against the Persian army and now one of the largest and most efficient container ports in Europe, should have provided some inspiration for Greece to better manage its economy going forward. Those expectations are unlikely to materialize.

Chapter 10

China

Most evenings after finishing his work shift, Li Jieming would glance through the windows of the bus taking him back to his dormitory to catch the neon-lit skyscrapers of Shenzhen's city center. He had been working in Shenzhen for the past 2 years, but his fascination for this bustling city had yet to fade. It felt like a completely different world compared to anything he had seen before. He was proud to be a part of it, contributing to a bright national future, however modest that contribution may be.

For the past 2 years, Jieming had been working in a factory that produces commercial vehicles on the outskirts of Shenzhen, a city of more than 12 million inhabitants, located to the north of Hong Kong and part of the Pearl River Delta, the largest manufacturing hub in China (and by extension, in the world). Now 25 years old, Jieming was born and raised in a village in Gansu province, not far from the Mongolian border, but more than 1,000 miles away from Shenzhen. Having completed 8 years of education, which by his own admission taught him very little, and having worked for a few years in the fields harvesting barley and wheat, he decided to leave his village in search of better pay and a better life. His wife, who takes care of their 5-year-old son together with her and Jieming's parents, works in a small garment shop in the village and complements her income with the monthly remittances that her husband is able to send back home.

Jieming's life is by no means an easy one. A typical workday starts at 7 am and finishes at 5 pm, 6 days a week. Overtime is expected whenever his company's order book increases. His dormitory and the neighborhood it is located in feel cramped compared to the wilderness of his village. He is entitled to few social benefits. Above all, he misses his wife and son, whom he sees once a year for a few days. Yet, despite the hardship, Jieming remains upbeat. He gets along well with his boss and colleagues, is grateful for the skills he has learnt, and his company has always paid him on time, which he was told is not always the case elsewhere. His wages have risen steadily over the past 2 years as his skills improved. He also feels generally accepted in the city despite his status as a migrant worker.

Jieming may be able to move back closer to his family in the near future. There have been more job opportunities in his province offering higher wages, although not as high as what he currently earns. A friend has put him in touch with a factory in Lanzhou, about 50 miles away from his village, which would allow him to spend more time with his family and see his son grow up.[1]

Jieming is one of 250 million migrant workers, more than the entire population of Brazil and twice the population of Japan, representing a sixth of China's overall population and more than a third of its workforce.[2] Migrants mostly originate from inland provinces in the north and the west who settle in the big cities along the coast in the east and the south that offer better opportunities despite higher living expenses. This is gradually changing as local policymakers are increasingly focusing on the economic development of the country's hinterland. Most migrants return home once a year during the Chinese New Year in what constitutes the largest human migration in the world. Their work is often menial and low paying and they have at times been neglected by urban citizens, but they have made an invaluable contribution to the economic rise of their nation, producing goods on an unparalleled scale through their indefatigable efforts.

Moving mountains

Countless books have been written on China's ascent. The factors underlying its success are believed to be institutional: market reforms and a focus on exports. Its authoritarian leadership is often seen as an impediment to growth: China would have grown even more rapidly had it adopted democratic institutions. Following that logic, other developing countries should replicate China's policies, preferably with a democratic regime in place, and they, too, would enjoy much higher standards of living.

China's meteoric rise since the 1980s has rightly been attributed to market reforms and opening up to the world. Those factors have had an enormous impact on the country. But they do not explain the *extent* to which China's economy has grown for more than 30 years. Many countries have implemented similar market reforms but did not see their economy double in size every 7 years or so over multiple decades. China could not have grown as much as it did without the inherent industriousness and thriftiness of its population.

Starting from a very young age, this focus on hard work, common in all Confucian societies, has allowed China to score very well in PISA education rankings, topping the charts in its latest edition. There is, however, a large contrast between large cities and the rest of the country. Whereas teachers in large cities are relatively well paid and well trained, rural areas struggle to attract competent teachers. While teachers are held in very high regard throughout China, low salaries and a lack of training facilities in rural areas have prevented those regions from advancing education levels as much as large cities have. Things have improved, with subsidies and other incentives provided to teachers to work in rural areas, but the gap with large cities remains.[3] Similar to other Confucian societies, students are put under enormous stress to succeed academically. The recent crackdown on private tuition and exam bans for those below the age of seven may reduce their workload and improve the prospects of poorer students who could not afford quality tutors. Anxious parents, however, are unlikely to reduce the pressure on their children to excel at school.

Various tales extolling the virtues of determination and perseverance are symptomatic (and not just anecdotal) of the importance of hard work. Virtually everyone in China knows the tale of 90-year-old Yu Gong, a man who lived in a remote village with two nearby mountains blocking access into the valley. He decided to remove the mountains and started carrying stones from the mountaintops every day, helped out by his friends and family. One day, a man who was puzzled and amused by what he saw, told Yu Gong that he would never be able to move the mountains, especially at his age. Yu Gong replied that he may be old, but he has children, who will have children themselves. His family will grow and grow and the mountains will become smaller and smaller. Eventually, the Gods in heaven were moved by such determination and took the two mountains away. The moral of the story is that with sufficient perseverance and hard work, anything is possible. China has been moving mountains for the past 30 years.

There is some evidence that the younger generation, who did not experience the hardship of their ancestors and who aspire to a more hedonistic lifestyle, may not be willing to put in as much effort. A 2005 survey showed that, in China, those who value hard work the most are the ones with the lowest income levels. The more a person earns, the less he will focus on hard work and getting rich, preferring instead to "lead a life that suits his tastes."[4] Often pampered and financially supported by their parents as the only child, millennials are part of a growing middle class that is increasingly shying away from a punishing work culture.[5] Still, hard work remains the norm in Chinese society.

Savers in the factory of the world

China's very high savings rate at 45 percent of the national income, one of the highest in the world, is due to several factors. The first is the one-child policy: Parents save more when they only have one child not only because their expenses are lower but also because in their old age they may have less financial support from their offspring. The desire to own a property is rooted in Chinese culture and forces people to save more, especially when real estate prices increase rapidly. Another factor is the fact that wage increases have not kept up with the country's productivity gains, increasing corporate savings. Weak social benefits are sometimes thrown into the list as well, but that is unlikely to be the case: Other countries with comparatively weaker social benefits do not have higher savings rates (most low-income nations, the UK, the US) and several countries with generous social benefits also have high savings rates (Nordic countries, Switzerland).

Thrift, in our view, also explains why households save as much as they do. That willingness to save has existed for a long time. In Confucianism, "frugality is a feature shared by virtue of every description; extravagance is the worst of evils."[6] People were unable to save much during the three decades following the 1949 Communist Revolution because their incomes were far too low. As the economy grew, people were able to save much more and align their actual savings rate to the one they desired, in part based on their level of thrift. An American missionary from the early twentieth century observed how "nothing is left unused. Entire animals would be eaten, with nothing thrown away. What cannot be employed in one place, is sure to be just the thing for another, and the least trifle of stuff is sufficient for the binding of a shoe."

The average foreigner was considered a "soap-waster." "The Chinese have such ingenuity in being able to re-use pretty much anything for other uses."

Savings make their way into investments, which represent about 42 percent of the GDP.[7] The country has grown by investing in property, infrastructure, factories, machinery, and increasingly research. Investments may be high, but during most years, they remain below what the country saves. As a result, excess savings are "exported" to international markets, generating large current account surpluses. Stated differently, if the country saves a lot, by definition it consumes less. Although consumption is timidly rising (more on that later), it "only" represents 55 percent of the GDP (compared to more than 80 percent for the US). Local companies therefore have to find markets outside of China to grow their operations. As the country opened up to the world and joined the World Trade Organization in 2001, exports soared as China capitalized on its cheap and industrious labor.

More recently, China has been "exporting" its savings through the Belt and Road Initiative (BRI), which consists of multiple infrastructure projects across various countries. With an overall cost estimated at close to a trillion dollars, it is a massive undertaking aimed at better connecting and stimulating growth in Asia and beyond, as well as further developing China's western and northern provinces. As countries involved in the BRI develop their infrastructure and a growing middle class emerges, this should ultimately increase demand for Chinese products and services. As China's own infrastructure has already gone through significant modernization efforts in recent years and returns on investment at home are in decline, the Belt and Road Initiative provides further opportunities (but also risks) for Chinese companies and banks to be involved in the upgrade of infrastructure in places where such upgrades are often badly needed.

Feeling the stones and catching mice

The greatest achievement of China's economy has undoubtedly been its successful transition from a planned to a market economy. Under the leadership of Deng Xiaoping, experiments with various pricing and production systems in the agriculture sector led to countrywide reforms that allowed farmers to sell their excess production at much higher prices and manage their own land. Manufacturing in towns became organized in newly created structures that specialized in various products. Those entities were gradually allowed to keep their profits and increase salaries, giving a higher incentive for employees to perform. Most of those companies eventually became privatized and provided much-needed competition not only among themselves but also to state-owned enterprises (SOEs). Starting in 1988, houses could be purchased and sold, paving the way to a flourishing property market. Entrepreneurs were given permission to start companies. Price controls were gradually lifted. A string of financial and fiscal reforms were enacted. Overall, the introduction of market principles has greatly improved the efficiency of China's economy.

A key aspect of this transition has been the *gradual* and *pragmatic* implementation of reforms, famously encapsulated in Deng's sayings: "crossing the river by feeling the stones" and "it doesn't matter whether the cat is black or white, as long as it catches mice." China saw what happened to Russia when it embarked on drastic "shock therapy" market reforms in the early 1990s after the fall of the Soviet Union, with large public assets sold to oligarchs for a pittance and the general chaos that characterized the economy during those years, culminating in Russia's default on its public debt in 1998. As journalist Arthur R. Kroeber has argued, "If state assets are privatized but competition mechanisms remain weak, the results will be poor: one just substitutes private monopolists or oligopolists for state-owned ones."[8] China was understandably not keen to follow that example, favoring an incremental approach, one less guided by ideological considerations. The country tested new ideas, implementing those that worked on a wider scale and ditching those that failed. This learning process was evident in the establishment of special economic zones in coastal areas, put in place to experiment further with market principles, attracting foreign investment by lowering trade barriers and capital controls and learning from superior foreign technology, not only in terms of products but also to improve operational and management processes. The special economic zones proved very successful and many of their features were expanded to the entire country.

This process of economic transformation was far from straightforward. Market reforms at the end of the 1980s, some of which were perhaps too drastic, not only unleashed strong economic growth but also led to fast-rising prices and at times arbitrary privatizations during which public assets were plundered by a few individuals. Inflation reached record levels, growth started to falter, and unemployment soared, leading to unrest. Many started to question the usefulness of reforms. It took a few years and a tour of Southern China for Deng Xiaoping and his followers to convince political leaders that returning to a planned economy was not a viable option and that China should push forward with reforms. Those events and the gradual approach that China favors for its reforms underline a major concern for the country that extends well beyond the economy: stability.

Stability and the role of SOEs

One remarkable aspect of China's growth has been its consistency: Whereas other countries go through booms and busts, China has so far had a very stable growth path. Cyclical patterns certainly exist and China's macroeconomic indicators are not always reliable, but the state has been instrumental in reducing cyclical movements by being proactive both in terms of stimulating the economy during downturns and preventing it from overheating. The idea behind those corrective measures has been that what matters most is stability, not growth at all costs. Growth is required, but uncontrollable growth is undesirable. Stability is also reflected in the continuity of the central government. China has shown that an authoritarian leadership, one which is not distracted by elections and is able to plan for the long run, is not an impediment to economic success, contrary to the view held by many in the West that democracy is a critical precondition to sustainable growth.

Economic stability is easier to achieve with a thrifty population and a reliance on investments. By increasing investments during economic downturns, the country has been able to stimulate the economy back on track. It does so by directing banks to lend more to SOEs (at very favorable rates) and SOEs to invest in various projects. Investment is easier to control than consumption. To stimulate consumption, people can be given an incentive to spend; but even then, the final decision rests with them. If they do not spend more, the impact of any economic stimulus is likely to remain muted. But with investments and in a country where an authoritarian government has control over banks and public companies, the state can have a direct impact on growth. Liquidity does not get "trapped" in the banking system or in companies as it has been for many years and to varying degrees in developed economies following the financial crisis of 2008. Aside from instructing banks to lend and SOEs to invest, China, just like any other nation, has other fiscal and monetary tools at its disposal to regulate market activity, including interest rates, bank reserve requirement levels, taxes, and import quotas.

SOEs play an important role in stabilizing the economy by investing at times when few are willing to invest and refraining from doing so at times when the economy is performing well. But they also represent a drag on the economy. Their executives are bureaucrats and party cadres who have little interest in growing revenues or increasing profits. Their salaries are capped and have in recent years been curtailed, giving them little incentive to outperform. Promotions and compensation levels are based more on the connections they nurture with other public officials and less on the way their companies are operated. They, therefore, have little incentive to become more efficient and innovative. Customer satisfaction with products and services offered by SOEs is generally low.[9] SOEs used to attract the vast majority of top university students, but have at times struggled to do so as more young graduates are joining private companies instead, lured by attractive packages and promotions based on merit.

SOEs benefit from many advantages over private companies. Permits for projects are fast-tracked; land can be acquired quickly and at cheaper rates; and funding from local banks is readily available and provided at very competitive rates. Private companies, on the other hand, in particular small and medium enterprises, struggle to secure funding from local banks or from underdeveloped capital markets. And yet, private companies are generally much more efficient than public ones.

The most successful attempt at reforming SOEs was at the end of the 1990s, when things came to a head. Large banks were awash with nonperforming loans, which accounted for as much as 40 percent of their total loans by the government's own admission. Premier Zhu Rongji, another towering figure in China's economic ascent, forced SOEs to let go of millions of workers, improve their efficiency, adopt international accounting standards, sell assets, and, for some of the larger SOEs, list on international exchanges. Zhu also increased the wages of public servants to reduce the incentive for them to collect bribes. Bad loans were transferred to newly created companies with the objective of disposing of those loans over time and recovering what could be recovered (some remain outstanding to this day). Timing was key: China's economy was doing well despite the Asian financial crisis and dismissed workers could find other jobs relatively easily. Those reforms would have been far more challenging if they had been implemented during a downturn. They worked: SOEs became more productive and banks improved their balance sheets. But within a few years, SOEs would fall back into their old habits.

If SOEs were managed like private companies, hiring the most qualified persons for each job and focusing on results with pay and promotion based on performance alone, they would be much less of a drag on the economy. The Chinese economy would likely grow faster if SOEs and banks were all privatized. But at the same time, the government would lose its ability to regulate the economy through cycles. It therefore has a delicate balancing act between full privatization of state companies, which would generate higher but more volatile growth, and reverting back to the preeminence of public companies with little room for private ones, a scenario that would seriously derail growth. The middle ground so far has been to try and make at least *some* SOEs more competitive and more efficient but continuing to use them extensively during economic peaks and troughs. This has worked well, but has also come at the expense of much higher debt and less productive investments.

Debt piling

A growing concern, both inside and outside China, has been the country's mounting debt levels. China sits on a large and increasing debt pile that may become unsustainable. Corporate debt levels and debt incurred by local governments are the main concern. Household debt is also rising, as higher property prices force people to subscribe to higher mortgages, but overall it remains well contained. Central government debt is also low. Those arguing that very high corporate debt levels in China could lead to a full-blown crisis too often ignore the fact that the structure of the Chinese economy is very different from that of other countries. Focusing on corporate debt in isolation makes little sense because it disregards the fact that many public companies are in effect an extension of the state. In most countries, a fiscal stimulus usually results in higher government debt, but in China that function is primarily performed by banks and SOEs, which are, respectively, instructed to lend and to invest. Two-thirds of corporate debt is held by SOEs.[10] As such, a more relevant metric to measure debt levels in China is the entire debt of the country, aggregating the ones held by households, corporates, financial institutions, and the government. Total debt stands at about 350 percent of the GDP. Compared to developed economies, the corresponding figures are 650 percent for Japan, 430 percent for the United Kingdom, 360 percent for both South Korea and the United States, and 260 percent for Germany. But China is still an emerging economy. Against countries of a similar level of development, China *is* heavily indebted. The total debt for Mexico, for instance, which has a similar GDP per capita as China, is only about 80 percent of the GDP.[11]

It was not always like that. Until 2008, overall debt in China was well contained as it represented less than 100 percent of the GDP, but it has since increased by 10–20 percentage points on an annual basis. Initially, this was a response to the 2008 global financial crisis that resulted in China facing much lower demand from the rest of the world for its products, forcing its economy into a slump. The stimulus worked, getting the economy back on track. But, since then, the growth that China has experienced in the past decade has been mostly debt-fueled. Not only has the overall amount of debt increased but the quality of that debt has also become more questionable. Local governments, which are responsible for most of the country's public spending, as well as SOEs have at times engaged in wasteful investments (roads to nowhere, ghost towns, and overcapacity in sectors such as steelmaking) fueled by credit in an effort to reach and exceed GDP growth targets. Those investments add little value and undermine economic stability by generating low returns or outright losses and non-performing loans. The much lower returns on assets by SOEs since 2010 are evidence that investments are not as efficient as they used to be.[12] China has generated "excessive growth" over the past 2 decades by directing capital to unprofitable projects for the sole purpose of generating higher growth.

Investments that were traditionally financed by loans from banks have increasingly been financed by the less regulated shadow banking sector. Shadow banking refers to intermediaries other than banks that provide similar financing services. In China, a wide range of companies are now involved in shadow banking, including large corporates, insurers, asset managers, and trust and leasing companies. One example is Alibaba's Ant Financial that provided, until recently, a wide array of financial services, including billions of dollars' worth of money transfers and loans. Investors are lured by higher rates of return compared to deposit rates from traditional banks, for a risk that often remains very low, but in some cases may be higher than investors realize. Insurers entered this lucrative business by offering investment products that sometimes had little to do with insurance. Shadow banking is believed to represent 25–30 percent of all banking assets in the country.[13] Local governments and banks themselves became regular users of shadow banking: Local governments had set up their own trust banks to increase their sources of funding, and banks offered various products referred to as wealth management products which were typically recorded off their books and as such evaded further scrutiny by regulators, in particular compliance with capital adequacy ratios.

There should, however, be little reason to panic. While the accumulation of debt is a cause for concern, it should not result in a large financial crisis. The government has historically pulled the breaks on overheating markets to ensure the overall stability of the system. Since 2017, it has cracked down on shadow banking, forcing banks to record wealth management products on their balance sheets and ensuring that

insurance companies focus on their main line of business. Shadow banking activity has since been reduced, from 87 percent of GDP at the end
of 2016 to less than 50 percent in 2021.[14] Overseas expansion by Chinese
companies, whether through acquisitions or organic growth, is now much
more closely monitored. Overcapacity in sectors such as steel and coal,
has been reduced and the monitoring of debt incurred by local governments has improved.[15] After years of strong growth, the property market,
especially in large cities, has been hit by cooling measures, restricting
lending into real estate and enforcing regulations for new constructions,
effectively slowing down speculative activity and the rise of property
prices. The government's track record is evidence that it will take further
action to prevent things from getting out of control and jeopardizing the
country's long-term stability.

Another reason why current debt levels will not lead to a full-blown
crisis relates to the structure of the economy, in particular the power that
the state wields over its banks and SOEs. Banks, which are almost all
state-owned, will not stop lending to each other and to SOEs. SOEs will
not stop investing if the state instructs them to continue doing so. Any
bank on the brink of collapse and posing a systemic risk will, in all likelihood, be rescued. The failure of one systemic bank would imply the
complete failure of the state, a highly implausible scenario. Consumption
could decline sharply and badly affect national growth rates, but a full-
blown financial crisis remains highly unlikely.

Other reasons sometimes put forth to dismiss alarmist views on
rising debt include high savings rates, the fact that virtually all the debt
is denominated in local currency, that the central bank can always step
in to provide liquidity, and that most of the liabilities of banks are deposits, which put Chinese banks in a safer position compared to US investment banks that struggled to refinance themselves during the 2008
crisis. But those factors would not by themselves prevent a financial
crisis. In the early 1990s, Japanese households held large savings

predominantly deposited in local banks; most of the country's debt was owned by the Japanese; and the central bank of Japan was able to step in to provide liquidity to the financial system. Yet, Japan still experienced a major financial crisis that led to a steep decline in consumption and investment.

People spending more, but slowly

Over the past decade, China has tried to move away from an economy fueled by investments and exports to one that is more consumer-driven. The need to "rebalance" the economy stems not only from rising debt and unproductive investments that are not conducive to sustainable growth but also from the need to be less reliant on foreign factors, such as the 2008 global financial crisis, the war in Ukraine, and the ongoing trade wars. An export-led growth strategy relies on global demand for Chinese products and services; that demand is volatile and difficult to control. Any swing in global demand directly affects local exporters and the wider Chinese economy.

But rebalancing the economy will take time. A thrifty population is not going to change its habits overnight. Policies aimed at reducing savings rates may have some short-term impact but are unlikely to permanently affect those savings rates. One structural factor with the potential to reduce savings rates is a rapidly aging population, as retirees are unable to save as much as they desire, which is the case in Japan and South Korea. But as discussed previously, in China, retirees continue to save a large portion of their income because most of them retain the *ability* to do so. They remain as frugal as they have been throughout their lives and benefit from financial support from their children and grandchildren. Many of them live with their family, in effect reducing their living costs to a minimum. An aging Chinese population is therefore unlikely to significantly reduce national savings rates in the near future.

Another structural factor that is starting to have an impact is consumerism by a new generation. Just like their counterparts in other countries, young adults are much more willing to spend than their parents or grandparents were. They are increasingly purchasing branded clothes, beauty products, and luxury watches, going to fine dining restaurants, acquiring a car, and traveling abroad, all of which end up on their social media profile and elicit the admiration (or the jealousy) of others. Social status, perceived or real, has become an important consideration not only for people's self-gratification but also to attract a potential partner. Short-term consumer loans have reached record highs in a country where it is relatively easy to obtain a loan through mobile phone applications, circumventing traditional banking channels.[16] We should, however, not conclude that young adults in China are becoming as spendthrift as their US counterparts. On average, they still save a much higher portion of their income. But they do spend more than their parents or grandparents did. As a result, consumption in China is rising and now represents the largest component of the GDP as well as the main driver of GDP growth. But the rise is a very gradual one and will remain so.

Moving up the value chain

After enacting sweeping market reforms and opening up to the world, China flooded international markets with cheap and functional products, quickly learning how to assimilate foreign technology and processes. It was able to produce and sell huge quantities of goods at low prices by establishing large factories that benefited from economies of scale and by relying on an almost endless supply of hardworking citizens joining factories from all over the country and willing to work for very low wages.

That workforce is no longer as cheap. Wages have been steadily rising as the economy expands and living costs increase, prompting workers to demand better pay. Nor is the workforce as plentiful in a rapidly aging population. An increasing number of foreign companies that had moved their production units into China, and also Chinese companies themselves, are now looking elsewhere (a trend that started before the ongoing trade wars). Countries such as India, Bangladesh, and Vietnam pose an increasingly strong threat to Chinese workers. Rising labor costs have also, similar to other nations, pushed Chinese companies to automate their processes.

As such, focusing on basic products is not the right strategy anymore because those products are becoming too expensive to manufacture in China. To remain competitive and provide work to the hundreds of millions of Chinese workers, China needs to move up the value chain. That means higher value-added products and services. Important progress has been made over the years. Gone are the times when "made in China" was synonymous with poor quality. Today, China produces a dizzying array of high value-added products: cars, computers, drones, satellites, and planes, to name a few.

Going up the value chain also means becoming more innovative. Science and technology are key areas of development for Chinese officials. With research and development (R&D) representing two percent of GDP, China spends less than the US but about the same as the EU. A record two million patents are approved every year. We should, however, remain cautious about those numbers that measure quantity, not quality. Much of the investment in R&D relates to the purchase of equipment that has so far seen little utilization. Three quarters of patents filed in China are weak, sometimes even worthless (known as utility and design patents as opposed to the more valuable invention patents) and primarily aimed at receiving subsidies. Many students graduate as engineers but only a few end up enrolled in real engineering work.[17] That said, progress has undeniably been made over the years. China ranked 11th in the latest Global Innovation Index, a significant improvement compared to 2013 when it ranked 35th. It has also become easier for entrepreneurs to start a new venture, with China now ranked 17th in the World Bank's index of starting a business as procedures have been simplified and the costs of registering a new company reduced, although this improvement in the rankings has been contested.[18] Generous grants have been offered to promising entrepreneurs and to Chinese academics from reputable universities around the world to return to China.

One area that is preventing China from becoming a truly innovative nation is intellectual property (IP) rights. Companies that are not protected and rewarded for their innovations will struggle to invest much in research and development. Why bother when innovative products and services can easily be copied by a competitor at little cost? IP rights do exist in China (they were put in place as early as 1985) and are not that different from those in other countries. The issue is that they are rarely enforced and penalties for violating IP rules are very modest and so do not act as a deterrent. The old habit of studying the technology of competitors and copying it remains the norm. China is understandably hesitant to truly crack down on IP violations given that weak intellectual property rules have benefited the country tremendously in past decades. Back in the 1980s and 1990s, there was little interest in developing brands or innovative products that Chinese consumers could not afford. It made more sense for Chinese entrepreneurs to copy foreign products and produce as many of those products as they possibly could. But as production costs rise, as the middle class grows, and as a younger generation is increasingly able and eager to spend, innovation will play a much more important role in generating future economic growth. That requires strong IP protection. Here, as well, progress has undeniably been made, yet IP protection continues to fall short of standard practices in higher-income societies.

Crooked beams

Intellectual property rights are only one aspect of China's judiciary. For businesses to prosper, they need to operate in an environment where rules and regulations are clearly defined and enforced. China's legal system has come a long way since the days of Mao. Toward the end of the 1990s and following a typically gradualist approach, experiments with the rule of law were conducted in cities such as Shenzhen, and then implemented nationwide. In the past few years, further efforts have been made to reinforce the country's legal framework. Those include better education and training of judicial appointees, standardization of laws across the country, enforcement of property rights, abiding by the constitution, cracking down on corrupt judicial officers, and appointments of local judges by the central government, not by local officials.

Despite those improvements, China's legal framework still has a long way to go. The country remains behind in its ability to enforce existing laws and protect investors, as compared to other countries. Companies have to navigate through multiple layers of overlapping regulatory bodies and a wide array of laws that apply to different sectors. It is true that the country has grown spectacularly in the absence of a strong rule of law. But as the economy moves up the value chain and China cracks down on corruption, a stronger rule of law will be required. Not only do arbitrary decisions impede the ability of companies to grow further but they also encourage corruption. Strengthening the rule of law is always going to be more difficult in the absence of an independent judiciary. SOEs should not receive preferential treatment in courts: In the long run, the absence of preferential treatment would actually work in their favor, forcing them to improve their operations and become more productive instead of relying on their privileges to fend off competition from the private sector.

Corruption in China has been widespread since the implementation of economic reforms, taking different forms over time, from the abuse of the dual-track price system in the 1980s to the smuggling of imported goods in the 1990s and the selling of public assets such as land, real estate, and natural resources for a fraction of their value from the 1990s onward. Things improved somewhat in the late 1990s and early 2000s as SOEs became more efficient and wages for public servants were increased, but the period that followed was marked by a resurgence of corrupt practices as many SOEs returned to their old ways as their managers at times complemented their revenues with illicit gains.

China's leadership is well aware of the risks posed by endemic corruption and has taken a strong stance against it. Thousands of public officials have been caught in the anti-corruption campaign that started in 2012, which often ended political careers and imposed lengthy jail terms. Many are now understandably fearful of committing such acts or even being perceived as doing so. It should be noted that those investigations have taken place outside the official legal system. Keeping a system clean must start at the very top; as a Chinese saying goes, "If the upper beam is not straight, the lower beams will be crooked." Yet, as China ranks 78th in the latest Corruption Perceptions Index, much more needs to be done to strengthen the rule of law and ensure higher transparency.

Markets in the balance

Ever since China began its economic revival, many in the West have been predicting its imminent downfall. They would observe the country's economic and political model, compare it to what they perceived to be the only path to sustainable growth, and dismiss China's economy as one that would inevitably decline if it did not conform to the predominant western consensus, in which democracy, civil liberties, and the withdrawal of the state featured as vital preconditions. As we write those lines, the expected economic boost following the lifting of

COVID-19 restrictions has not materialized, several large defaults in the real estate sector have taken place, and youth unemployment is hitting record highs.

Gloomy observers were (and still are) making two mistakes. First, a strong government and an authoritarian regime are no impediment to growth, as long as market principles, including fair competition and a level playing field between participants, are upheld. The technical know-how displayed by China in high-tech sectors, such as space flight, electric batteries, photovoltaics, and machine learning, is clear evidence that a country can harness cutting-edge technology without democratic institutions. London School of Economics Professor Keyu Jin economics Professor Keyu Jin points out that China "built the world's fastest supercomputer, first solar-powered expressway, conducted the first 5G-enabled remote surgery and is moving ahead of the US in internet- and perception-based AI, digital payment, quantum communication and speech technology, including English."[19] Second, most observers dismiss the idea that human values play any role in economic growth, yet cannot provide an explanation as to why poor Chinese migrants eventually enjoy higher standards of living compared to local populations wherever they relocate, or why savings rates are so much higher in China compared to other countries with similar low levels of social protection or demographic trends.

The greatest threat to China's continued economic success is not the absence of a liberal democracy, nor is it trade wars, a rapidly aging population, high levels of debt, or the inability to move up the value chain. Some of those challenges can certainly lead to slower growth. Yet none of them looks insurmountable to a Chinese leadership that has systematically and aptly responded to them, not only learning from the rest of the world but also pursuing its own approach, such as its policy of strong intervention in weathering economic cycles that could serve as a model for other nations. The main threat to the Chinese economy would be to roll back the gradual market reforms implemented over the past three decades, reneging on market principles that have transformed its economic landscape. If commercial decisions are progressively made by officials with little understanding of and little interest in the operational performance of the companies they monitor and if private companies are increasingly crowded out and disadvantaged against public ones, it will inevitably lead to lower productivity, lower growth, and *higher* instability. When it comes to economic decisions, a pragmatic approach will always work better than an ideological one; catching mice with white cats alone will yield inferior results. Private companies have contributed the most to the growth of the economy, have created the most jobs, and are much more technologically driven than SOEs. Yet they struggle to obtain funding for further growth, especially following the crackdown on shadow banking. Cracking down on the excesses of shadow banking was a positive development to maintain stability, but local banks need to provide funding to private companies, and not just to the biggest ones.

SOEs have the potential to become more efficient and market-driven while remaining under the control and ownership of the government. At times when economic cycles lead to excesses, whether booms or busts, the government should continue to play an active role in the lending policies of banks and investment policies of SOEs. But at other times, government intervention should be minimized to ensure the optimal allocation of resources through market forces. Singapore's model of state ownership with minimal interference in the running of government-linked companies can serve as an inspiration, perhaps with a more proactive role for the Chinese state during more volatile times. It is not an easy balance to strike, but one that is essential for the continued growth and stability of the economy.

If market reforms are not reversed, the future for China looks very bright. With a hardworking and thrifty population, it is unlikely to fall into the middle-income trap that has affected so many other emerging countries. Despite inevitable bumps along the way and a society that will have to become more innovative and consumerist, China should continue to rise and eventually reach standards of living comparable to the wealthiest nations.

Chapter 11

Russia

The 1990s are known in Russia as *likhiye devyanostyye*, the "wild nineties." Most Russians had their first taste of rock and roll music, bubblegum, and McDonald's burgers. Large quantities of chicken thighs were imported from the US, quickly becoming known locally as "Bush legs" in reference to the US president at the time, each the size of an entire Soviet chicken. The opening of borders saw the emergence of "shuttle traders," people making short trips to purchase products from abroad and sell them locally. Youths wearing red jackets and gold chains around their necks, showing off their newfound wealth often acquired through dubious ways, were a common sight on the streets of Moscow. Criminal gangs and scams proliferated. A popular joke back then was that capitalism was the exploitation of man by man, whereas communism was just the opposite.

This was a decade where Boris Yeltsin cemented his power in 1993 by ordering tanks to shell the country's parliament building, killing 187 people. Never shy of controversy, Yeltsin was once found clad only in his underwear along Pennsylvania Avenue during a 1995 visit to Washington, trying to hail a cab and insisting on ordering pizza.[1] It was not the first time Yeltsin was found inebriated in his underwear. In 1989, he had to account to the highest legislative body of the Soviet Union on how he ended up at a police station outside Moscow dripping wet and almost naked. He said he was attacked, with his head covered by a sack, and dumped off a bridge into a river. Top communists at the time said he had been drunk while on his way to a tryst with a lover. Other gaffes include pinching the backside of a secretary in front of cameras and failing to emerge from his plane at a stopover in Ireland in 1994, leaving his hosts stunned on the tarmac.[2]

But perhaps the most famous anecdote about Yeltsin was when he and his team were sailing down a Siberian river on a triple-decker riverboat. Vyacheslav Kostikov, the press secretary, was bothering the President with his banter until Yeltsin could stand it no longer and told three of his biggest aides to toss the troublesome spokesman overboard. This is how Alexander Korzhakov, Yeltsin's former chief bodyguard, recounts the incident:

> "One of the aides graciously suggested: 'Vyacheslav, take off your shoes. They're expensive Italian ones, you'll wreck them.'
>
> 'It's fine, don't try and frighten me,' parried Kostikov.
>
> 'Throw him,' the President ordered and they calmly tossed him overboard.
>
> Thankfully, they gave him a good swing — the top deck was much narrower than the middle or lower one. Had they simply dropped Kostikov over the side, he could have broken his head open. At that moment I was standing on the second deck admiring the Siberian scenery. Suddenly Kostikov flew past me, his arms and legs jerking desperately. At first, I took him for an enormous bird, but an instant later I recognized the familiar bald head and dashed up to the third deck. The press secretary was fished out of the water, found to have a bump on his head and revived with a flask of vodka."[3]

Keen to secure reelection in 1996 despite low approval ratings and deteriorating health after a series of heart attacks, Yeltsin sold large public assets to a group of well-connected and wealthy individuals in exchange for their financial support, in effect monetizing state assets to finance his campaign. It worked: Yeltsin was reelected. Yet, 2 years later, Russia would default on its international creditors, plunging the country into a deep crisis that had many longing for a return to a more stable and predictable communist era.

Chaos and permanence

Russia's contemporary history has been a tumultuous one. Whereas other formerly planned economies such as China, Vietnam, and India have favored a gradual transition toward free markets, Russia underwent radical changes in the 1990s, shaking the very foundations of Russian society.

Change back then was a necessity. The Soviet Union was disintegrating after decades of economic stagnation and mismanagement. Its leaders at the time made the brave decision to break with the past and adopt a completely new economic model. But they had very little experience or understanding on how to proceed. They looked to emulate the West, forcing the mantra of free markets and democratic ideals onto a society that was ill-prepared for it. The expectation was to transition from communism to capitalism, but instead, the country descended into anarchy. Public assets were sold to a small group of individuals for a pittance. Hyperinflation wiped out savings. Between 1991 to 1995, GDP dropped 34 percent, more than US GDP during the Great Depression of the 1930's.[4] Life expectancy decreased and crime rates went up.[5] Despite the economic hardship, some Russians look back at the 1990s with fondness, an era of freedom that they had never experienced before. But for many others, particularly older generations, it felt confusing and humiliating as the nation was forced to cede a large chunk of its territory and adopt a system and lifestyle imposed by their triumphant historical foes.

Vladimir Putin, who became president in early 2000, brought the chaos to an end by ushering in much needed stability. Whereas his predecessor had appointed no less than five prime ministers in the previous 4 years, the same prime minister remained in place during Putin's first 4-year presidential term. Several far-reaching reforms took place during that period. A major tax upgrade in 2000 simplified the tax system, reduced tax evasion, and improved tax collections from regional states. Private property rights were better recognized and new bankruptcy laws put in place. Judges were given more independence, especially from regional state authorities. Juries were established for the first time in 2003, improving the fairness of trials.

The sale of public assets for a fraction of their value in the 1990s did have one positive outcome that would become apparent years later. Those companies that were badly managed under Soviet rule became much more efficient under private ownership. This was especially true in the oil and gas sector, which saw a significant rise in production levels during those years. Oil revenues increased not only because of higher volumes but also because of higher prices. Russia was, and still is, highly dependent on oil prices, which reached a record high in 2008. But it would be wrong to attribute almost a decade of prosperity solely to higher oil prices. This was as much driven by commodity prices as it was by political stability and structural reforms. From 2000 to 2008, Russia's average annual growth was 7 percent. Productivity grew by 6 percent annually. GDP per capita went from $9,300 in 1999 to $21,600 by 2008. Russia's share in the world economy grew fourfold. Public debt and inflation were reduced significantly.[6] All those indicators admittedly started from a very low base following the chaotic 1990's. But they do reflect an era of renewed optimism and rising living standards.

Crowding out

Since the 2008 financial crisis, however, Russia's economy has faltered. Nominal GDP plunged 9 percent in 2009 and has only grown by an average of two percent each year since 2010. With inflation rising by 5 percent on average during the same period, most Russians have seen their real income reduced. Because the slowdown in Russia after 2009 was much more pronounced compared to other oil-producing nations, lower growth in the country cannot be solely attributable to lower oil prices.[7] More recently, Western sanctions and the war in Ukraine have, further aggravated the country's economic performance.

The decline in living standards in the years following 2008 was expected in the aftermath of the financial crisis and fall in oil prices. Much less expected was the anemic growth that has persisted for over a decade. Two-thirds of Russians are no better off today than they were in 1991.[8] GDP per capita in Russia is less than half what it is in Estonia, and only a fifth of what it is in the US. In 2020, China's GDP per capita overtook Russia's, implying that the average Chinese citizen is now richer than his Russian counterpart. Russia continues to be heavily dependent on the price of its natural resources despite efforts to diversify the economy. Yet even during years such as 2014 and 2018 when oil prices rose, the economy hardly picked up.

Prior to the war in Ukraine, the main issue that was plaguing the Russian economy in the past decade, much more so than a declining population, Western sanctions, and lower oil prices, was the *crowding out of the private sector*, a vital sector without which sustainable growth is all but impossible. Too many private companies in Russia are unable to operate in an environment that would allow them to grow their operations. Many of them, especially profitable ones, are forced to comply with unreasonable tax demands or other forms of extortion. The tax police, fire inspectors, financial regulators, and other officials prey on successful private businesses to obtain their share of a company's earnings. A successful entrepreneur quickly becomes a target. Between 2003 and 2013, it was estimated that one in every six businessmen in Russia faced some form of prosecution.[9] Access to capital is also a struggle for private companies, as Russia's mostly state-owned banks lend primarily to state-owned companies at subsidized rates.

Private companies are often barred from competing with or dealing with public firms. An increasing number of sectors are monopolized by state-owned companies, preventing the entry of competitors and providing no incentive for the state companies to become more productive or innovative. Some of them continue to operate despite heavy annual losses, manufacturing shoddy products, or delivering substandard services and are kept artificially alive by the state for fear of a public outcry should those companies be wound down, preventing stronger competitors from replacing them.

Since the mid-2000s, the state has steadily increased its presence, partly driven by the wish to have national champions. A 2019 study by the International Monetary Fund (IMF) estimates that the state accounts for almost half of all employment and a third of the GDP in the country.[10] The presence of state-owned companies itself is not the issue. It was never an impediment to the success of China, Singapore, and a few other countries. The issue is the inability of private companies to grow and compete against them. As former Finance Minister Alexei Kudrin described it in a 2014 article, "The problems of the Russian economy are of a persistent nature and cannot be resolved with simple measures such as softer monetary or budget policy. The fundamental reason for these problems is the weak market environment dominated by public and quasi-public companies, which are guided by a substantially distorted motivation, that is, they are less interested in earning a profit, and their commercial activity is often combined with the actual function of a 'government agent'. They are less liable for their performance results, as losses can be covered by the state."[11]

The absence of fair competition hampers entrepreneurship, innovation, productivity, and ultimately growth. Firms have little incentive to manufacture better products or provide better services. The country's productivity, measured in GDP per hours worked, is only half of the OECD average and has been steadily declining since the mid-2000s.[12] A 2009 McKinsey report found that Russia spends less than half of the OECD average on research and development, and of the little that it does spend, around 70 percent is public spending. The report goes on to say that only one in ten Russian firms reports any kind of technological innovation activity, compared to between three and four firms out of ten in OECD countries.[13] With few opportunities to innovate and be rewarded for their efforts, many of Russia's brightest minds migrate to places where their skills will be better recognized.

When trust fails

The difficulty in establishing a vibrant private sector is compounded by the prevalence of corruption, itself the result of low levels of trust Russians have for each other. According to surveys, only 23 percent of Russians trust other people.[14] One possible explanation is the environment of constant suspicion that characterized Soviet rule. Back in those days, state informers were everywhere. Most communal apartments had at least one *stukach*, a person whose role was to inform the state of any perceived wrongdoing.

Low levels of social trust have led to high levels of corruption. The country ranks 137th in Transparency International's latest Corruption Perceptions Index, alongside Gabon and Mali.[15] In a 2011 survey, 7 percent of Russian firms claimed that private gifts and payments made by firms in order to affect laws, decrees, and regulations had a "major" or "decisive" impact on their business, compared to 2–3 percent in 2005 when the previous survey was conducted.[16] Low trust also leads to a more unequal society. Russia ranks as the 80th most unequal nation in the world, as measured by its GINI coefficient. But it is in terms of wealth that inequalities are the most pronounced, with the one percent of

Russia's wealthiest believed to own 60 percent of the country's total wealth, one of the largest proportions in the world.[17]

Russians are unlikely to become more trusting of each other anytime soon, so that is not an option to reduce inequalities. Higher rates of taxation are unlikely to increase tax revenues for the state in a country where many transactions are done on the black market and wealthy individuals establish their fiscal residency in jurisdictions beyond the reach of local tax authorities. As a result, Russian society will remain highly unequal.

Some progress, but…

A more dynamic private sector and a real crackdown on corruption should be a catalyst to much stronger growth and finally allow the country to detach itself from the gyrations of oil prices.

In addition to the political and economic stability that the country has achieved since the chaotic 1990s, Russia can also rely on a highly educated workforce, ranking 32nd in the latest PISA rankings, higher than Israel or Iceland.[18] The country has pioneered several innovations, in sectors such as aeronautics, semiconductors, chemistry, and software. Russia and the Soviet Union have amassed 31 Nobel prizes, the seventh highest globally, mostly in mathematics and physics.[19] The state has benefited the most from this collective knowledge, predominantly its space program and military sector.

But this knowledge has so far failed to translate into practical innovations for local companies because of weak governance, a lack of access to funding, and weak intellectual property rights. There may also be a negative attitude toward the commercialization of innovative ideas.[20] Russia's schools and universities are far superior to many other nations at a similar stage of development. This heritage is, however, going to waste when many of Russia's brightest emigrate and when local companies are unable to transform innovative ideas into tangible products and services that create jobs, generate taxes, and ultimately contribute to a stronger economy. The state sought to remedy this situation by opening a large technological park outside Moscow in 2009, the Skolkovo Innovation Center, aiming to become Russia's Silicon Valley. While the park has expanded to a combined $1.4 billion in revenue, it has fallen short of expectations, attracting only $200 million in annual investments, and has been embroiled in various corruption scandals.[21]

One metric where Russia has undeniably made progress is the Ease of Doing Business rankings compiled by the World Bank, where the country moved from 124th in the world in 2010 to 28th in 2020, a remarkable achievement (China ranked 31st and was accused of inflating its own numbers). Russia joined the World Trade Organization (WTO) in 2012 and has made great strides in terms of contract enforcement, property registration, and starting a business. It has become easier to start a business and enforce contracts, but the reality is that too many private companies continue to struggle in an environment of rampant corruption and unfair competition from state-owned companies. More than half of business owners believe it was easier to do business in the 1990s than it is today.[22]

Fate over destiny

To better understand Russia's economic woes, we need to delve deeper into Russian values, in particular its work ethic. Seventy years of communism had removed almost all incentive to work hard in a system where the state pretended to pay workers who pretended to work. Irrespective of how industrious a population may be, a system that removes any incentive to perform is bound to fail.

But when that system is replaced by one which does provide better incentives to work harder, societies where hard work as a value has been ingrained in people for centuries are expected to become much more productive. China operated as a planned economy for 40 years; yet its citizens rediscovered their Confucian work ethic when the country transitioned toward a market economy. Even 70 years of communism under Soviet rule could not completely suppress prior attitudes toward work. A 2001 survey in Latvia, a nation with a predominantly Protestant heritage, asked respondents to choose between three statements: "1. Work is a moral necessity; industriousness will give you success and prosperity." "2. Work is a hard necessity of life. Extra work is evidence of greed." "3. Work is a way of getting money; the best job is that which gives much money with minimal work." 76 percent of Latvians chose the first statement, in line with their Protestant heritage. But the same survey done in Russia showed that only 53 percent of Russians chose the first statement. 32 percent of Russians chose the last statement (the one about minimal work), compared to only 17 percent of Latvians. Although Russia and Latvia were both members of the Soviet Union and under communist rule (in the case of Latvia, from 1941 to 1991), those different responses reflect different values transmitted from one generation to another.[23]

Orthodox Christianity, the most widely professed faith in Russia, contends that there is nothing that a believer can do to earn salvation. This is in stark contrast to Protestantism where hard work and materialistic success are considered important steps (or signs) toward salvation. Similar to Catholicism, the belief of the Russian Orthodox Church that our fate in life is sealed provides far less of an incentive for people to work harder.

This to some extent explains the fatalism that is so common in Russian society. Most Russians believe in luck and fate more than the idea that hard work would yield a better outcome. In a World Values Survey, 44 percent of Russians believed that hard work usually brings a better life, compared to 65 percent in both the US and China.[24] A tale taught to all young Russians is that of Ivanushka Durachok, a fairytale hero who is often described as competing against his two elder brothers and succeeding in life, not through hard work, but because of luck and his good nature. He marries the tsar's daughter in one episode and lives in a palace. He wishes nothing more than to laze around, reinforcing the belief that no matter the actions that we take, they will have little impact on our lives. Russians use the word *avos'* to describe a philosophy that treats life as inherently unpredictable and where one can only rely on luck. It also explains the rather indifferent attitude of Russians toward COVID-19 where many shunned measures such as mask-wearing and social distancing.[25] In his book *Ecce Homo*, Friedrich Nietzsche describes "Russian fatalism" by giving the example of a Russian soldier who, "finding a campaign too strenuous, finally lies down in the snow. No longer to accept anything at all, no longer to take anything, no longer to absorb anything — to cease reacting altogether." Another example of Russian fatalism can be found in Mikhail Lermontov's novel, *A Hero of Our Time*, where the main protagonist, an army officer by the name of Grigory Pechorin, is constantly bored despite the life-threatening situations he finds himself in, disillusioned with life and convinced that his behavior merely reflects fate. The lack of a strong work ethic constitutes an obstacle to higher economic growth, whatever the policies put in place. Better policies will improve Russia's standards of living, but the country is unlikely to reach the levels achieved by more economically developed nations.

Expecting the unexpected

A strong Russia requires a strong Russian economy. And a strong Russian economy is only possible with a strong and vibrant private sector. Political stability, achieved over the past two decades, will be difficult to maintain in the absence of economic growth. The same holds true for military power. The war in Ukraine has exposed the frailties of Russia's underfunded armed forces.

In recent years, Russian authorities have looked toward China for inspiration on what economic model to follow, growing increasingly suspicious of the West's insistence on democracy, human rights, and privatization. Similar to Russia, China is a stable authoritarian nation with several large companies owned by the state, playing an important role in their respective sectors and benefiting from cheap financing from state-owned banks.

Yet China's economic growth has outperformed Russia's every year in the past two decades and its citizens are now more prosperous than their northern neighbors. There are two main reasons for this. First, the private sector in China has been allowed to thrive. State-owned companies in China, for all their flaws, often compete with private firms and therefore have a higher incentive to perform. China has been much more successful than Russia in its fight against corruption, at least at the corporate level. Second, the Chinese have, on average, a higher work ethic, which, given the right incentives, results in higher productivity.

Without a vibrant private sector, Russia's economy will be unable to replicate the strong growth it enjoyed in 2000–2008 and will continue to depend heavily on commodities, mostly oil and gas. This creates large swings over time, with periods of stronger growth followed by periods of economic decline, threatening the stability that Russia's aging population treasures above everything else. Older generations often lament the fall of the powerful Union, reminiscing about an era where schools, medicines, and hospitals were free and rents were cheap. Life was more simple back then. The younger generations, which grew up in a post-Soviet world, often have higher aspirations than their parents or grandparents did. But fate alone will not suffice for those aspirations to be realized. With little hope of improving economic prospects in the long run, fatalism and passivity are likely to remain core features of Russian society.

Chapter 12

Oman

In the early 1990s, one of the writers of this book (Thomas) was on a road trip with his father Pierre, mother Monique, sister Nathalie, and grandmother Dory across Oman, a country located on the southeastern coast of the Arabian Peninsula and home to 5 million people. Thomas was about ten years old at the time with his sister being 2 years younger. After spending a few days in the capital city of Muscat in the north of the country, his parents rented a car for a 600-mile trip across the Rub' Al-Khali desert, a virtually uninhabited desert among the driest in the world. After 2 days of driving and sightseeing, the plan was to reach Salalah, a coastal city in the south, not far from the Yemeni border. The family left around 9 am on a beautiful day without a cloud in the sky. Despite the remoteness of the area upon leaving Muscat, the road was in good condition.

A few hours into the trip, a loud noise brought the occupants of the car out of their reverie. At first, no one understood what had happened, but as Pierre was having difficulties steering the wheel, it became clear that one of the tires had a puncture. Stopping the car by the roadside, Pierre went out to inspect the damage. The expletive he uttered made Thomas realize that this was a serious issue. Pierre then went to open the trunk, which contained a replacement tire. The problem was that neither he nor anyone else had any idea how to replace a tire. An instruction manual was provided, both in English and Arabic. Pierre tried to do what the manual said, loosening the lug nuts and lifting the vehicle off the ground, but he was growing increasingly impatient and clearly struggling.

As Pierre and Monique began to argue over what to do next, Thomas gazed into the desert. The beautiful scenery of endless sand dunes was beginning to look much more intimidating. His parents' arguing contrasted with the eerily silent desert. No other car had been encountered in the past hour or so. It was approaching noon and temperatures were rising fast. Dory remained in the car, not quite sure what to think of all of this and probably wondering whether it really was such a good idea to accompany the family on this trip. The brick-sized mobile phone in the car was of little use without satellite reception.

"Dad, are we going to die?" asked an anxious Nathalie.

"No honey, we're not going to die" answered Pierre, trying to reassure his daughter.

"Look, there's a car coming!" shouted Monique, pointing toward the section of the road that the family had come from. Everyone looked up. It was only a small dot on the horizon, but it was getting bigger. It turned out to be a pickup truck. Thomas's parents did not waive their hands or seek the attention of the driver in any way, probably a bit embarrassed by their predicament and believing they could eventually sort it out by themselves, but the pickup truck slowed down anyway as it got closer and eventually came to a stop. The driver came out and walked toward the stranded family. Smoking a cigarette, he could not have been more than 15 years old. He looked at the punctured tire and, without saying a word, started working on it. He clearly knew his stuff. Within just a few minutes, the tire had been replaced. Each family member looked at him with astonishment, as he completed his task with so little effort when it had seemed nearly impossible to them.

"See Dad, that wasn't so hard after all!" Nathalie taunted her father, who chose to ignore her.

Pierre then hurried back inside the car to collect his wallet and reward his young savior, handing him several banknotes. The young man shook his head, put his thumb toward his mouth and uttered the very first word since he arrived: *water*. Surprised, Pierre went back to the car and gave him two big bottles of water. The boy nodded his appreciation, went back to his car, and drove off.

To this day, Thomas remains amazed by the boy's behavior. He could have purchased many more bottles of water with the cash that was handed to him. He certainly did not seem desperately thirsty. But his priorities laid elsewhere. It was not about accumulating cash, but about what he wanted the most at that particular instance. Most of us grow up in materialistic societies, where the pursuit of money is an end in itself. This is also true for Oman. But as we will see throughout this chapter, it is perhaps less true in Oman compared to many other countries. Most Omanis do not define their happiness by the amount of money or other material possessions they own. A successful life to them has much more to do with family, friendships, religious faith, and tolerance toward others.

From one young savior to another

Oman's modern history can be traced back to the early 1970s when Sultan Qaboos, with the help of the British, took over from his father in a bloodless coup, exiling his father to London where he would spend the last 2 years of his life in a suite at the Dorchester Hotel. Back then, the Sultanate of Muscat and Oman, as it was called, was a shadow of its glorious past, when the Omani Empire in the nineteenth century controlled large swathes of modern-day Iran, Pakistan, Yemen, and much of the coast of Eastern Africa. By 1970, the country had been closed to the world: Citizens were barred from traveling abroad and any foreigner seeking to enter required the personal consent of the Sultan.[1]

Most people depended on subsistence farming and fishing for their livelihood. Few buildings had electricity. Only three primary schools (for boys only) existed, whereas regional neighbors such as Saudi Arabia, the UAE, and Iraq had set up a large network of schools more than a decade earlier.[2] The entire road network had only six miles of paved road and only 840 motor vehicles were registered.[3] Oman has discovered oil in 1964 and started producing it in 1967; however, production remained low. Various separatist movements threatened to overthrow the monarchy. Qaboos's father had started behaving in a rather erratic manner in his last years of reign, banning the use of radios, forbidding citizens from wearing sunglasses, and forbidding people from talking to one another for more than 15 minutes.[4]

On the day he acceded to the throne, 28-year-old Qaboos declared, "Yesterday it was complete darkness and with the help of God, tomorrow will be a new dawn on Muscat, Oman and its people."[5] That is exactly what happened. Over almost 50 years of reign, Sultan Qaboos opened up and modernized his country. Roads, airports, and seaports were built and expanded. Private companies were allowed to compete with public ones. Education, healthcare, and pensions all improved dramatically. Life expectancy rose by 30 years. Oman has transformed itself over those five decades. Its GDP per capita, around $15,000, is double that of Botswana or Brazil, and five times greater than that of Egypt, Tunisia, Algeria, or Morocco. In 2010, the United Nations ranked Oman as the country that had developed the most over the previous 40 years, ahead even of China (admittedly starting from a very low base).[6]

But the greatest achievement of Sultan Qaboos, one that most enabled a rise in standards of living, has been the use of Oman's oil reserves. Supported by foreign technical expertise, production quickly ramped up in the 1970s, at a time when oil prices were surging. Sultan Qaboos ensured that oil revenues would be invested in better infrastructure and social services, ultimately benefiting a large portion of the population, including tribes living in the interior of the country, away from the more affluent coastal areas.

Oman has benefited greatly from its oil resources, becoming highly reliant on them. Numbers have varied over the years depending on prevailing oil prices, but oil typically represents half of the national GDP, 60 percent of exports, and 85 percent of government revenues.[7] Similar to Botswana and its reliance on diamonds, this oil dependency also means that the country's economic fortunes fluctuate with oil prices: When oil prices go up, Oman thrives; when they go down, the economy suffers.

Rentier state

Oman is a member of the Gulf Cooperation Council (GCC), a political and economic union that comprises Saudi Arabia, Kuwait, the UAE, Bahrain, Qatar, and Kuwait. The policies implemented by each of these countries have been fairly similar. Each one is ruled by successive generations of the same family and each has become highly dependent on oil for its prosperity. Income taxes are very low or nonexistent, while education and healthcare are free. Another commonality among GCC members is the predominance of the public sector: Most large companies are owned by the state.

For all its progress, Oman has not become as wealthy as other Gulf states, relative to its population. Saudi Arabia, Bahrain, Kuwait, and especially Qatar and the UAE are richer. The main reason is that Oman has fewer oil reserves compared to these countries. Because oil revenues are lower, there is less money available to build more schools, universities, and hospitals, to provide comfortable pensions, or to attract foreign investments. In the cases of the UAE and Bahrain, their efforts to become international financial centers have also contributed to their growth.

The wealth generated from oil revenues is of a very different kind compared to countries without large natural resources. This is because wealth, in the form of oil reserves, already exists within the country. It does not need to be "created." As long as Oman and other Gulf countries continue to extract oil from the ground and sell it for a decent price, whether in crude or refined form, and as long as oil revenues are distributed to their wider population, these nations should continue to prosper.

The oil bonanza had an unintended consequence. Omanis have little reason to work hard. They do not need to. They expect the state to take care of them throughout their lives — free education, free healthcare, a well-paying and secure job in one of the many state-owned companies upon graduation, generous unemployment benefits, no taxes, and comfortable pensions. This is sometimes referred to as a rentier state, where citizens benefit from rents generated through oil revenues even though those citizens contribute very little to the actual generation of those rents.

The work that does need to be done is delegated to migrant workers. In the case of Oman, they account for more than half of the working-age population, a common feature across Gulf states. Migrants range from low-paid, low-skilled workers, mostly from South Asia, employed in menial or physically demanding jobs that Omanis are unwilling to do, to highly skilled, highly paid workers, often from high-income countries, with specific skills that locals lack. In effect, there are two job markets: one for locals and one for migrants, with little competition between those two groups. A vast majority of Omanis prefer to work in the public sector, whereas most of the migrants are employed in the private sector.

Economists tend to look down on such a system. They argue that, to move forward, a country needs to become more productive, more innovative. They advocate for a more competitive marketplace and will often favor the removal of ruling families and their replacement with elected leaders. But, is that really necessary or even desirable? Even though the political system adopted by Gulf countries is very different from most Western nations, it works just fine as long as revenues from natural resources are maintained (more on that later). Gulf states have achieved a high level of development under a stable leadership that caters to the needs of their population. Oman would be wealthier if its population worked harder and its economy was more productive, competitive, and innovative. But, would it really be worth it?

Ultimately, we all strive to have a happy and enjoyable life. According to surveys, Omanis are a happy bunch. They rank 22nd in the World Happiness Report (all Gulf countries rank in the top 50).[8] Omanis may not be as rich as Singaporeans or Americans, but they lead a life that they are mostly contented with. They do not have to worry about good grades at school, stress at work, losing their job, devoting too little time to their families, or collecting pension in their old age. Most of them are able to spend as much time as they want in practicing their religion and interacting with families and friends. Family ties are very important to Omanis and throughout the Middle East. Most Omanis may work in bloated and inefficient public companies, but that in itself has not stopped the country from reaching a high level of development. Oman's economy is far from innovative; instead, new technologies are imported from abroad, which has so far worked just as well. With a life expectancy of 78 years, the average Omani lives as long as the average American. Would becoming richer make Omanis happier? Not if it implies giving up the quality of life they have enjoyed in the past few decades. Income inequalities are also relatively low, with a GINI coefficient similar to that of France or Germany.[9]

Beyond oil

The biggest threat to this system, of course, is that it relies on oil revenues remaining high for the foreseeable future. In the case of Oman, time is running out. The country produces less than 1 million barrels of oil each day, compared to 3 million barrels for Kuwait, 4 million barrels for the UAE, and more than 12 million barrels for Saudi Arabia. Several Omani oilfields are fast becoming depleted. The few new ones are difficult to access. Oil reserves, at 5 billion barrels, are expected to last just another 25 years (by comparison, Kuwait's reserves are estimated at more than 100 billion barrels and Saudi Arabia's at more than 250 billion barrels).[10]

The current economic structure that Oman has relied on for the past 50 years and which has transformed its society may no longer be sustainable. Without oil, the system collapses. The state will simply run out of money if it maintains spending at current levels. It may be able to continue borrowing for a few more years after oil runs out, through capital markets, fellow GCC states, China, the IMF, or other international lenders, but that will not prevent Oman's financial situation from deteriorating further. Eventually, the state will be unable to cover persistent losses generated by inefficient public companies, maintain its existing infrastructure, and provide the same social protection to its citizens. Budgets will have to be cut. Oman's finances are already in a precarious state as few reserves have been accumulated at times of higher oil prices. The country's sovereign wealth funds hold assets valued at less than $50 billion, compared to more than $800 billion for both Kuwait and Saudi Arabia, and $1.5 trillion for the UAE.[11] The ability of Oman to maintain a fixed exchange rate with the US dollar (all GCC members have pegged their currency to the US dollar) will become increasingly difficult.

Local authorities are well aware of the need to diversify their economy away from oil. One option has been to replicate what has been achieved with oil to other natural resources found in the Sultanate, such as gas, mining, and fishing. Oman started to produce and export gas in the 1990s, mostly to South Korea. Although copper has been extracted from the Omani ground since prehistoric times, production has only really ramped up in recent years. New mining regulations were introduced in 2019 in a bid to attract more foreign expertise and capital into the sector. As for fisheries, increased investments have lifted local production and exports.

Unfortunately for the country, there is not enough gas, copper, or fish available to replace oil. Oman's gas reserves are among the smallest in the region and only a fraction of Qatar's, the world's largest gas producer.[12] The same holds true of copper, zinc, and other metals, currently comprising less than 2 percent of GDP and unlikely to go much beyond that. Overfishing will eventually lead to fewer fish in the area, but even without overfishing, this is a sector that will never contribute to a large portion of the country's economy.[13]

Other ideas have been explored. Setting up an international financial center in the capital city of Muscat by wooing international banks and other companies will be difficult to achieve given the regional competition of Dubai. Tourism has also been touted as a potential growth market. Oman is a beautiful and safe place to visit. Natural sites include mountain ranges, canyons, and oases. A rich architecture and culture and, perhaps most importantly, the warmth of the Omani people represent other selling points. Oman attracts 3.5 million tourists every year. But just like gas, mining, or fishing, tourism will not be able to replace oil.

The only real alternative to oil is to make the economy more productive and more efficient. One promising venture has been to set up a regional logistics center, connected by road, ship, air, and rail. The aim is to leverage Oman's strategic location as a gateway to the Indian Ocean and at the crossroads of Southern Arabia's ancient caravan routes. The Governorate of Musandam overlooks the Strait of Hormuz, a shipping lane through which countless containerized shipments and 90 percent of the Gulf's oil exports transit. A 425-mile highway linking Oman to Saudi Arabia across the treacherous dunes of the Rub' Al-Khali desert, inaugurated in December 2021, should boost trade and tourism between the two GCC countries by cutting travel time from 18 hours to 6 hours. Several free trade zones have been set up, allowing for 100 percent foreign ownership and providing various benefits, such as exemptions from taxes and customs duties, cheaper financing, and subsidized land and electricity. Ports are being expanded. For example, the port of Salalah, already a large container port, is aiming to become a transportation and storage hub for chemicals, food processing, warehousing, and liquid bulk storage. In time, Salalah will be connected to the Gulf Railway, a planned railway network linking all six GCC countries. Authorities are developing an air cargo corridor for the country, mainly for the purpose of facilitating exports. The University of Muscat launched a faculty for transport and logistics in 2017 to equip young Omanis with the necessary skills to navigate those growing industries. Oman is also betting on manufacturing, including chemicals, plastics, furniture, paper products, and textiles. These industries are currently in their infancy; the challenge will be to further develop them. This will not be easy given strong competition from Asian and other GCC countries.

The country offers a stable and safe environment for companies to operate in, but not one devoid of corruption. The country ranks 69th on the Corruption Perceptions Index, similar to most other Gulf states but better than the Arab nations in North Africa. It lags behind the UAE (27st), which instituted stronger reforms to fight corruption in a bid to attract foreign investment. Connections (known as *wasta* in Arabic) are essential to conduct business, find a job, or speed up documentation. Someone who hails from a well-connected family will have a definitive advantage over someone who does not. Overall though, existing levels of corruption should not be a deterrent to foreign companies looking to enter the local market or local companies looking to further develop their operations.

Another area where more could be done is the participation of women in the workforce. Much progress has been made since the early 1970s when girls were barred from attending school. Women now have the same access to education as men. They obtain higher grades and graduate in higher numbers than men from Omani universities.[14] But at the same time, the proportion of women in the workforce, below 30 percent, is one of the lowest in the Gulf.[15] As a result, many female graduates do not use the skills they acquire during their studies. Cultural factors are also at play. Women often stop working after getting married (the decision to abandon their job is not always theirs to make). They prefer shorter working hours and overwhelmingly favor the public sector. Ensuring that more educated women join the workforce and remain in it would undoubtedly increase the nation's productivity.

A thorny transition

The various measures outlined here go in the right direction, but they will not be sufficient for Oman to maintain its current standards of living. Quitting its addiction to oil implies a radical transformation of Oman's society, one that cannot simply be done by way of economic reforms, but one that requires a change in mindset. No longer will Omanis be able to rely exclusively on the state for their well-being. They will have to work for it. Wealth will need to be created, not just extracted from the ground. As author and energy expert Daniel Yergin commented in reference to GCC economies, "The value system has to shift away from a system based upon entitlements and subsidies to one based upon performance, competition, and delivery, and one much less dependent upon government decision making."[16] Without oil, companies in Oman will have no choice but to become more productive, more efficient, and more innovative. This requires an industrious workforce.

For those new industries to grow, a new attitude toward work is essential. Oil has probably had a bad impact in this respect, removing the incentive to work hard. But even without oil, those attitudes are unlikely to change. Other Arab nations with few oil reserves, such as Morocco, Tunisia, or Egypt, have been unable to increase their productivity over time to levels achieved by more developed countries.[17] A Gallup survey showed that 56 percent of Arabs in the Middle East and North Africa (MENA) region do not work, the highest proportion anywhere in the world, with 37 percent of respondents saying that they do not work because they do not want to.[18] Implementing the right policies and reforms will improve productivity, but not to the level of nations with a more industrious population. Morocco, Tunisia, and Egypt are 4–5 times poorer than Oman, as measured by their GDP per capita. There is a real risk that Oman's economy will decline toward those levels. Diversification is not happening fast enough. The highway linking Oman to Saudi Arabia was originally planned to be completed in 2014. The Gulf Railway was due for completion in 2018, but will take several more years to be completed. Several other projects announced 10 or 15 years ago have seen little progress.

This lack of progress amid declining oil revenues is creating discontent among Omanis. They are realizing that the cradle-to-grave state support they have enjoyed for decades and that they had taken for granted is coming to an end. Young Omanis (the country's median age is just over 30) are particularly incensed. Many of them are well educated and expect to start their career in the corporate world in a position of authority, dismissing job offers that do not correspond to their expectations. They often grow disillusioned by the strict hierarchy in public companies, having to report to older, sometimes less well-educated superiors. Youth unemployment in Oman is over 20 percent, not because there are no jobs around, but because young Omanis tend to be very selective with the jobs they want to do.

They can no longer afford to be as selective or expect the state to cater to all their needs. It is a change that is not easy to accept. The sporadic protests that have taken place in the past few years, including in 2011 in the wake of the Arab Spring, have been about economic demands, not political change. The ruling monarchy continues to enjoy strong legitimacy and has been a source of stability in a rather volatile region.

The state has tried to address these concerns by forcing companies, both public and private, to hire more locals, accelerating an "Omanization" policy that began in the 1980s. Such a policy has merit if locals are competing with migrants for the same jobs. By prioritizing access to some jobs to local workers, those locals should acquire better skills. Yet the results have been, and will be, disappointing: Omanis are usually uninterested in or underqualified for many of the jobs handled by foreign migrants. Few Omanis wish to join the private sector, which they consider to be exploitative, with longer hours and often less pay than the public sector. Locals fill up less than 20 percent of private sector jobs.[19] Forcing underqualified people into certain jobs further reduces the efficiency of those companies.

A closely watched neighbor

Similar to other Gulf countries, Oman has developed itself beyond recognition by making the most of its natural resources. Those resources are often a curse when they are badly managed, but they have been a blessing to Oman, providing a quality of life to its people that would not have been possible otherwise. Oil has acted as a shortcut to their prosperity. Little effort was required to achieve that prosperity, an option that is unavailable to nations devoid of natural resources.

As oil runs out, Omanis are unlikely to change their values, in particular their attitude toward work. This means they will have to make do with less. However, they may not necessarily become less happy if their life priorities do not revolve around materialistic gains. Some view their Bedouin roots with a hint of nostalgia, longing for older times. Yet the increasing frustration felt by many young Omanis in response to their leaders' timid but necessary economic reforms and budget cuts is a sign that once people get used to higher standards of living, it is difficult for them to make do with less.

Despite its relatively small size, Oman has played an outsized role in regional politics. The Islam practiced in Oman, Ibadism, is neither Sunni nor Shi'a, the two major denominations of Islam which have often been at odds with one another in the region. Sultan Qaboos was careful not to take sides or involve Oman in regional conflicts. This neutral position enabled the country to act as a trusted mediator. The evolving situation in Oman, both economic and political, will be closely watched by its regional neighbors. Because of higher oil or gas reserves, most of them can afford to delay painful reforms. But, ultimately, their economic model will also need to be adapted to a world keen to rid itself of its oil dependency.

Conclusion

In this book, we have explored how the interplay between human values and policies has resulted in vastly different outcomes for 12 countries, in terms of their ability to generate wealth and distribute it among their populations. By focusing on the human dynamics behind pure economic data, we have tried to offer a different perspective. China's incredible surge is rarely associated with the hard work and thriftiness of its people. Nor is Japan's anemic growth associated with the reluctance of its citizens to take risks, Sweden's egalitarian society associated with high levels of trust, Nigeria's economy associated with the hardworking and entrepreneurial Igbo, or Russia's stagnation associated with its people's enduring fatalism. By looking at countries through the lens of human values, we see different global trends emerging, which we summarize in this concluding chapter.

A tripolar world order

The world economy, which since the fall of the Soviet Union has been dominated by one superpower, will gradually move toward a system dominated by China, India, and the US.

The greatest strength of both China and India is a huge, hardworking, and thrifty population, enabling a much higher growth potential and ensuring that they do not become stuck as middle-income countries. The main threat to their success would be the removal or decline of market forces, reverting back to how their societies were structured before the reforms of the 1980s. That is unlikely to happen: Few would want to return to those days of autarky, stifling regulations, and even famine, especially those that have lived through them. But it is a possibility that cannot be ruled out entirely. Ideology is one of the greatest threats to progress.

China is already a superpower in its own right. The size of its economy is rapidly approaching that of the US. As standards of living improve, growth has inevitably slowed down in the past decade. But growth should remain sustained for the foreseeable future. As costs increase, Chinese products and services will move up the value chain. We see no reason why its citizens cannot become as wealthy as those in Japan or South Korea within the next 20–30 years.

Including India in this group may seem like an odd choice. Until very recently, India's economy had been growing more slowly than China's. Painful reforms still lie ahead to free up market forces, especially in agriculture and manufacturing. Despite the many problems that India is faced with, we believe its potential has barely been tapped. We expect the country to become the third largest economy in the world in the coming decade (it currently ranks 5th behind the US, China, Japan, and Germany). It might well surpass the US within the next few decades. One can only imagine where China and India would be today if they had not mismanaged their economies for multiple decades.

The US has a much smaller population compared to China and India: Chinese and Indians are about four times more numerous than Americans. The US economy is also much more developed: The average American is six times richer than the average Chinese and 30 times richer than the average Indian. Both factors (a smaller population and an already whigh level of development) limit America's further growth. But it will undoubtedly remain a very strong power. The view of many in China of a declining America because of a perception of political chaos and a workforce that may not be as hardworking as the Chinese is misplaced. The US economy will remain one of the most competitive and innovative for many years to come.

The stability of a multipolar world will depend on how those nations, each armed with nuclear weapons, will be able and willing to work together as well as with other countries. The US will have to come to terms with the fact that it cannot convert or control China or India. As for China and India, their growing influence around the world comes with greater responsibilities. Their legitimacy as global superpowers is yet to be achieved in many parts of the world. The misguided so-called wolf warrior diplomacy that China has adopted in recent years has been highly detrimental to its global image and will take years to rectify.

BRIC(S): A flawed concept

In 2001, Goldman Sachs economist Jim O'Neill coined the BRIC concept, identifying four countries with large populations and at a similar stage of development: Brazil, Russia, India, and China. The expectation was that each of those countries would eventually join the ranks of highly developed nations. BRIC became a formal institution in 2010, its leaders meeting regularly. South Africa was later included, making it BRICS. There have been various talks of including other nations such as Indonesia, Mexico, or Türkiye.

But the BRIC(S) concept was always flawed. O'Neill never considered the values of the people in those countries and especially their attitude toward work. China and India have a very high potential because they have a population willing to work harder. Brazil, Russia, and South Africa do not. The latter countries can certainly grow further, but will likely remain trapped as middle-income countries, never reaching the status of highly developed nations.

India is by far the poorest of the BRIC nations relative to its size. The GDP per capita in India is only a fourth or a fifth of what it is in Brazil or Russia. But given its much higher potential, and assuming it pursues the right policies, India should become wealthier than those nations much more quickly than is commonly assumed.

We should stop talking about the BRIC(S) nations. BRIC leaders themselves are not clear on what brings them together and how they should carry that organization forward. They seem aligned mainly in terms of their opposition to western powers more than any real factor that truly unites them.

Getting the right policies in place

Since the fall of the Soviet Union, nations rarely get their policies *completely* wrong. Almost all of them have adopted a market economy, at least to some extent. The planned economies in China, India, the Soviet Union, and countless other countries in Asia, Africa, and Latin America that destroyed the lives of millions are a thing of the past, hopefully permanently so. A market-based economy has made people wealthier, better educated, and able to live longer and in better health. Developing countries, on average, have never been richer.

North Korea and Venezuela (and Cuba to a lesser extent) are contemporary reminders of what happens when market forces are suppressed. The standard rhetoric by their leaders that their nation would be a socialist paradise if not for crippling western sanctions and western cultural influence fails to convince a population faced with continuous hardship, except for its most ardent ideologists. Sanctions are detrimental to economic activity, but they are not the cause of those countries' struggles. Those regimes are a painful but useful reminder of what *not* to do. Any leader tempted by such a model should realize the immense suffering it will impose on its people.

Although most countries no longer completely mismanage their economy, some still get many of their policies wrong. Sometimes, they borrow and spend beyond their means, as seen in the case of Greece. Or, they do not spend enough, favoring austerity at times when tepid growth would require more stimulus. Some, like Zimbabwe or Lebanon, get their monetary policies wrong and watch helplessly as their domestic currencies lose most of their value. Military coups are less common, although Thailand, Egypt, Sudan, Mali, Chad, Myanmar, and Afghanistan are reminders that they still take place. Those isolated cases, however, rarely result in a permanent state of decline. As long as decision-makers are not ideologically inclined to push forward with unreasonable policies, they are usually able to reverse course when the negative consequences of their actions become all too clear.

There are four specific issues that many countries struggle to resolve. The first is corruption, which is endemic in too many emerging markets. As levels of trust deteriorate (see next section), corruption is likely to expand further. For corruption to decline, several factors (willingness and ability from political leaders; effective rule of law; providing credible alternatives to bribes; and high transparency) need to occur *at the same time*, something that is very difficult to put in place. Every leader claims he or she will fight corruption; even when the intention is there, the results are often lacking.

The second long-standing issue is rising inequalities. This is also related, to some extent, to a loss of trust. The global corporate tax agreement in 2021, where 130 countries agreed to a minimum corporate tax rate, goes in the right direction. But much more will need to be done.

The third is the predominance of the public sector and the crowding out of the private sector. Most emerging countries have a large public sector. As we have seen, public companies can (and in some cases should) play an important role, but they need to be held accountable for their actions. Too often though, a lack of accountability results in a bloated and inefficient public sector, employing too many workers who generate too little output. When the public sector becomes too large, private companies will struggle to compete against it, either because they are not allowed to do so or because they do not benefit from the same advantages as public companies, such as cheap financing, subsidies, and access to customers or suppliers. This has been the case in Russia, in the Gulf states, in many Mediterranean countries, and elsewhere. China is also at risk of crowding out its private sector. Even Singapore, which manages its public companies better than most, at some point had too many of them and had to backtrack.

The fourth issue, perhaps the most urgent one, that many countries struggle to resolve, is climate change, which affects all of us and requires a global coordinated effort. The US, China, and India are the three biggest polluters on the planet. Lofty commitments by political leaders and senior executives over very distant future dates and significant uncertainty as to whether those commitments will be honored, are unlikely to be sufficient according to most climate scientists. According to a recent survey of 10 countries, more than half of the world's youth believes that the human race is doomed.[1] Not everyone is gloomy about the state of our planet. Massachusetts Institute of Technology (MIT) economist Andrew McAfee, author of *More from Less*, argues that the US is now using fewer natural resources than it did in the twentieth century, even though consumption has continued to surge forward. Products have become much more efficient, using fewer inputs for higher outputs. According to McAfee, the developed world is generating less pollution, and as lower-income countries develop further, they, too, should reduce their pollution over time. He advocates for more taxation of carbon emissions and better use of nuclear energy.[2] Whatever your opinion on climate change and how to resolve it, discussions around it are bound to take on ever greater importance.

A global loss of trust?

The trust that people have in others has deteriorated significantly in some parts of the world over the past 50 years. This has been particularly true for both the US and the UK, for reasons already mentioned. Elsewhere, social trust has not deteriorated as much, but it has declined to *some* extent. Surveys show that young people are less willing to trust others compared to their older counterparts, which hints toward a further decline of social trust going forward.[3] Trust in institutions is generally lower than it used to be, although that trust tends to be more volatile and can therefore rebound more easily than the trust we have for others.

We see trust in others declining further over the years, especially in developed countries and fast-developing ones where inequalities are rising quickly. People see others getting much richer than them, which can elicit envy, resentfulness, and anger. They end up losing trust in others and in their society. COVID-19 will have exacerbated those trends, as those with a secure and well-paying job accumulated savings during lockdowns, while others in low-paying jobs or those who lost their job during the pandemic struggled to make ends meet. Once it is lost, trust in others is unlikely to be recovered. Unfortunately, few policymakers devote much attention to maintaining high levels of trust. Few political leaders mention it, let alone make it a priority. But over time, trust is essential for a nation to function properly.

Trust in others is not only among citizens of the same country but also about trust in the people of other countries. Globalization should have brought people together by increasing interactions and making the world a smaller place, yet it seems to have had the opposite effect. Globalization has led to tensions. Migrants have increasingly been targeted, deemed responsible for many of the problems faced by locals, further reducing trust among different communities. Nationalism has grown almost everywhere. Locked borders due to COVID-19 reduced global interactions and made people more suspicious of others.

Rising global tensions

On 14 March 2020, a family of three, including two children aged two and six, were shopping in a store in Midland, Texas, when 19-year-old Jose Gomez lunged at them, armed with a knife. He stabbed all three, badly cutting the faces of the father and the 6-year-old son, including a cut to the son that reached from behind his ear all the way across to his eye. The suspect indicated that he stabbed the family because he thought they were Chinese citizens looking to infect others with the coronavirus. The family members were in fact Asian Americans who had settled in the country for many decades.[4] The start of the pandemic coincided with a sharp increase in discrimination and xenophobic attacks on East Asians in the western world, both verbal and physical.

At around the same time, foreigners living in Guangzhou, China, were seeing major shifts in the attitudes of the local population toward them. Matt Slack, a White man from New Jersey, described how he was refused entry to restaurants, how locals were unwilling to share the same lift or sit next to him on the subway.[5] Yet this was nothing compared to the plight of thousands of Africans living in the city, predominantly from Nigeria. Many were made homeless, forced to abandon their homes by landowners and local authorities. Some had to sleep on the streets for days, refused access to restaurants and supermarket chains, struggling to feed themselves.

Political leaders have done little to reduce tensions between countries in recent years; in fact, it has been quite the opposite. In the US, the virus has been repeatedly referred to as the "China virus," effectively blaming China for the havoc that COVID-19 has wreaked on the country. For its part, China has made unsubstantiated claims that the virus found on imported frozen food was evidence that its origins are to be found, not in Wuhan, but outside China's borders. Anti-China and anti-Western rhetoric and a rise in nationalism will do little to mend ties.

We should bear in mind that the behavior of a few does not extend to an entire population, that the misdeeds of some individuals are not representative of a larger society. The reality, at least in our experience, is that most people will do what is right by showing empathy, respect, and kindness toward others. In Guangzhou, local volunteers helped out Africans evicted from their homes. Many of those volunteers rallied to connect African workers with landlords and hotels and offered them counseling services. In Midland, Texas, Mr. Gomez was unable to carry out his objective of killing an Asian American family due to the intervention of a brave store worker who was able to wrestle him to the ground, take the knife out of his hand, and hold him until police arrived. It is those anonymous benefactors, not the ones guilty of transgressions, that should be making the headlines.

Women's untapped potential

In virtually every country, girls perform better at school than boys, across all grade levels and academic subjects.[6] It starts from a very young age: Girls in kindergarten, on average, pay more attention and are more self-disciplined than boys.[7] According to one study, girls are more adept at "paying attention to a teacher rather than daydreaming," "choosing homework over TV," spending almost double the amount of time doing homework, and "persisting on long-term assignments despite boredom and frustration."[8] By putting in more effort, girls obtain better grades. Why girls are more conscientious and work harder is unclear. Social, cultural, and biological factors are probably all at play.

It is not only in primary or secondary school that girls outperform boys. In most countries, they are also more likely to enroll into university.

University enrollment rates for women in emerging countries tend to be lower, but they too have been rising fast and should continue doing so. According to the World Bank, the proportion of women in post-secondary education for all countries combined went from 10 percent in 1975 to 20 percent in 2001, and accelerated further to 43 percent in 2022.[9] Increasingly highly skilled women enter the workforce every year.

Too often though, the skills they have acquired go to waste. Many well-educated women will be unable to contribute as much as they could to the growth of their country because of discrimination and other factors. Women often face discrimination when applying for a job or a promotion. They become stuck in roles that do not make full use of their skills. They are more likely to leave the workforce, because of frustration at their workplace, a lack of support in raising children, or other life priorities. Lower-income countries have much lower female workforce participation rates, in part because of cultural factors. In the Arab world, two-thirds of all women remain outside the workforce.[10] The work they do at home should be better valued (it is not captured in economic data such as GDP), but it is often work that does not make the best use of the skills they acquired during their formative years.

Much has been done to ensure that women are more highly educated. But more needs to be done to promote the participation of well-educated women in the workforce. This is especially needed in lower-income countries, where promoting women to positions aligned with their skills and their willingness to work hard represents a real opportunity to improve productivity. Women are also deemed to better manage the wealth of their household, as seen in the case of conditional cash transfers in Brazil and other countries that have implemented such programs. They are less likely to spend their income on frivolous items and go into debt. A higher savings rate for low-income families is often the first step toward reaching the ranks of the middle class.

A future for the world's children

Let us conclude with those who will shape tomorrow's world. Children are at a stage in their lives where they acquire values that are likely to remain with them for their rest of their lives. Whereas adults will rarely ever change the values they acquired during childhood, children are still trying to make sense of their environment and figuring out what values they identify with most strongly.

The ability and willingness to work hard is one of those values that parents and educators can transmit to children. It has the power to change their lives. The introductory quote of this book ("If you put in an enormous amount of work, you're going to have a tremendous advantage over people who don't.") is by Thomas Sowell, an American economist who has written extensively about culture and values. As obvious as that statement may be, it holds a lot of wisdom. Children who work hard may not succeed, but at least they are giving themselves a much better chance of obtaining better grades, higher educational degrees, better skills, a more fulfilling job, and greater wealth. There, however, has to be a balance. Kids can be put under enormous pressure to succeed, which can backfire, affecting their mental and emotional well-being. But *some* level of hard work will be invaluable to their lives. Too often, people realize in their 50s or 60s that they could have accomplished more by paying more attention in school and being more diligent in completing their homework. By then, it is often too late. Children may not enjoy those long hours of studying, but they will be grateful later on in their lives, knowing that their parents always had their children's best interests at heart.

This notion of balance, of not pushing toward one or the other extreme, applies to other human values as well. Children should learn about financial literacy and the role of savings. If later on in life they systematically spend all their income or go into debt, they may struggle to accumulate sufficient wealth to live comfortably. But at the same time, they should not aim to save all of their income. That would make for a rather joyless life. Besides, an economy could not function properly if everyone saved as much income as they could. Likewise, some risks should be taken in life. Taking risks all the time is unlikely to succeed, but always playing it safe prevents us from moving forward. As for trusting others, in general, the more trust, the better. But blindly trusting others is not advisable, as some people may take advantage of that trust. People should generally be trusted, but there are some people who probably should not. We have focused on hard work, thrift, trust, and risk-taking because we view those values as having an important role in the material well-being of people. But other values are just as essential for children to find their way in a complicated world. Kindness, honesty, justice, love, respect, curiosity, and empathy matter just as much to enjoy a more fulfilling life.

Endnotes

Front Matter

1. Thomas Sowell, Wealth, poverty and politics: An international perspective, 2015.
2. 1984 interview, *Tony Brown's Journal*.

Introduction

1. In Values at the core, we cited the following two studies: Joan Cost-Font, The cultural origin of saving behavior, 2018. Nicolas Fuchs-Schündeln, Paolo Masella, and Hannah Paule-Paludkiewicz, Cultural determinants of household saving behavior, 2017.
2. For an overview of the relationship between social trust and COVID-19 deaths, see Bernard H. Casey, COVID-19: Did higher trust societies fare better? March 2023.
3. Kyeyoung Park, The Korean American dream: Immigrants and small business in New York City, 1997.
4. Jean Tirole, Economics for the common good, 2017.
5. U.S. Census Bureau 2022 Educational Attainment.
6. 2022 American Community Survey.
7. Pew Research Center 2019. See also Jennifer Lee and Min Zhou, The Asian American achievement paradox, 2015 and Philip Kasinitz, John H. Mollenkopf, Mary C. Waters, and Jennifer Holdaway, Inheriting the city: The children of migrants come of age, 2009.

8. Amy Hsin and Yu Xie, Explaining Asian Americans' academic advantage over whites, 2014.

9. Another factor was a belief that certain minorities exhibit a higher cognitive ability for education. This explanation has since been dismissed. See for example Amy Hsin and Yu Xie, Explaining Asian Americans' academic advantage over whites, 2014.

10. 2019 American community survey, *Pew Research Center*, 2019.

11. Amy Hsin and Yu Xie, Explaining Asian Americans' academic advantage over whites, 2014.

12. Thomas Sowell, Intelletuals and Race, 2013.

13. Real median household income for Blacks was $45,422 in 1999 and barely above $46,000 in 2019, before COVID-19. Current population survey annual social and economic supplement historical poverty tables.

14. B. Rose Huber, COVID-19 shutdowns disproportionately affected low-income Black households, *Princeton University*, 30 November 2020.

15. There is an ongoing debate, stretching over decades, as to whether cultural factors may explain the higher income of American Blacks of West Indian descent compared to US native-born Blacks. We believe the main factor explaining that difference is a positive selection process, whereby many West Indian Blacks migrating to the US are already well educated and form part of the middle or upper class in their country of origin. Sociologist Suzanne Model has compared the income levels of West Indian Black migrants to native-born Blacks who have recently moved from one part of the country to another; she found similar income levels between the two groups, meaning that those native-born Blacks who are able to move around enjoy higher income levels, similar to West Indian migrants. Suzanne Model, West Indian migrants: A black success story? 2008.

16. 2022 American Community Survey.

17. Amy Chua and Jed Rubenfeld, What drives success? *New York Times*, 25 January 2014. It should be noted that the figure dates from 2013; to the best of our knowledge, more recent data on the ethnic composition of Black students at Harvard Business School are unavailable.

18. Thomas Sowell, Intelletuals and Race, 2013.

Chapter 1

1. The Guardian, 'Carnival of democracy': Celebration returns to Rio after a two-year hiatus, 6 February 2023.

2. *BBC News*, Brazil's samba schools go political as funding cuts bite, 9 February 2018.

3. MartketWatch, Rio's Carnival: Not just a local party anymore, 13 February 2012.

4. Werner Baer, The Brazilian economic miracle: The Issues and the literature, 1976.

5. United Nations conference on trade and development, commodity dependence: A twenty-year perspective, 2019.

6. Marcelo Dias Carcanholo, Orthodox economic policies of the Lula administration, 2006.

7. *The Economist*, The 50-year snooze, 19 April 2014.

8. Sérgio Buarque de Holanda, Roots of Brazil (Raízes do Brasil), 1936.

9. Echoes of slavery in the Brazilian work ethics, 27 August 2014, Institute of Advanced Studies of the University of São Paulo.

10. *Seattle Times*, Culture clash complicates China's Brazil push, 28 May 2011.

11. World Values Survey, percentage of those who believe that "Most people can be trusted," Waves 5 and 7.

12. Brazilian Institute of Public Opinion and Statistics (IBOPE), Retratos da Sociedade Brasileira: Confiança Interpessoal, 2014.

13. Alex Cuadros, *Brazillionaires*, 2016

14. *Transparency International*, Corruption perceptions index 2022.

15. There is an ongoing debate on the merits of conditional cash transfers (CCTs) versus unconditional cash transfers (UCTs). While both CCTs and UCTs provide benefits to the poor, CCTs are likely to be more effective than UCTs in most cases, even though they are more costly to put in place. For a non-technical overview, see *World Bank Blogs*, How should we design cash transfer programs? 6 February 2020.

16. *The World Bank*, Bolsa Família: Changing the Lives of Millions in Brazil, 22 August 2007.

17. Alan de Brauw, Daniel O. Gilligan, John Hoddinott and Shalini Roya, *The Impact of Bolsa Família on Schooling*, 2015.

18. Sofia Segura-Pérez, Rubén Grajeda and Rafael Pérez-Escamilla, Conditional cash transfer programs and the health and nutrition of Latin American children, 2016.

19. *Reuters*, Brazil boom lifts millions into middle class, 9 July 2008.

20. Statistics on the GINI coefficient in Brazil, IPEA (Instituto de Pesquisa Economica Aplicada).

21. *The Economist*, Bolsa Família, Brazil's admired anti-poverty programme, is flailing, 1 February 2020.

22. *Reuters*, How Ford burned $12 billion in Brazil, 20 May 2021.

23. *BBC News*, Brazil's business labyrinth of bureaucracy, 17 May 2012.

24. *The New York Times*, Always the Country of the Future, 23 July 1995.

Chapter 2

1. Ties will improve with mutual visits: Teng, *The Straits Times*, 13 November 1978.

2. Gross domestic saving as a percentage of gross domestic product, *The World Bank*. This very high savings rate should be interpreted cautiously: The number is distorted by the fact that only 60 percent of the annual GDP is generated by Singapore companies. The balance is produced by foreign entities who only consume a small portion of that income in Singapore, thereby artificially raising gross savings rates. It therefore makes more sense to consider the proportion of the GDP generated by Singapore companies that is not consumed. This results in a gross savings rate of 38 percent, still a very high figure but lower than what the official number suggests. The *Yearbook of Statistics Singapore* stopped publishing indigenous GDP figures in 2013. In 2015, indigenous GDP was SGD 240 billion at market prices, according to the Ministry for Trade and Industry (Parliament Q&A from 10 Oct 2016) against SGD 408 billion of GDP. Indigenous consumption is private consumption (SGD 150 billion in 2015) multiplied by the proportion of Singaporean residents in the overall population (70 percent in 2015) plus public

consumption (SGD 43 billion). This equates to 62 percent of indigenous consumption, or 38 percent of indigenous saving. All figures are from the *Yearbook of Statistics Singapore 2017*. See also Toh Mun Heng, High savings rate, but S'poreans are no misers, *The Straits Times*, 29 March 2011.

3.   Yearbook of Statistics Singapore 2017.

4.   Cheng Han Tan *et al.*, State-owned enterprises in Singapore: Historical insights into a potential model for reform, 2015.

5.   Carlos Ramirez and Ling Hui Tan, Singapore, Inc. Versus the Private Sector, Are Government-Linked Companies Different? 2003.

6.   Biotech sector poised to deliver more health and wealth, *Straits Times*, 29 July 2017.

7.   Lee Kuan Yew, 8 November 1993 speech for the "Africa Leadership Forum in Singapore."

8.   Private schools mainly cater to international students, religious groups and persons with disabilities.

9.   Copying allowed and can do even better, *The Economist*, 1 September 2018.

10. *Channel News Asia*, 476 suicides reported in Singapore in 2022, 1 July 2023.

11. TALIS survey, 2013, based on lower secondary teachers.

12. 2018 median income for Singaporeans and permanent residents was SG$53'244 (*source*: Incomes in Singapore up, with median salary rising above S$4,400: MOM report, *Channel News Asia*, 23 November 2018). Average starting salary for secondary school teachers in 2018 was S$68'954: Teachers in Singapore command high pay but work long hours, says international survey, *Today*, 8 November 2018.

13. Programme for International Student Assessment, 2018.

14. *Ministry of Finance*, 2019 figures. See also Balancing social spending with financial prudence, *The Straits Times*, 30 April 2018.

15. Lee Kuan Yew, The search for talent, 1982 speech.

16. Lee Kuan Yew, Singapore-UK relations: Bringing forward an old friendship, 2004 speech.

17. Lee Kuan Yew, From third world to first, 2000.

18. Housing and Development Board, Annual statistics 2018. Department of Statistics Singapore, Households, 2018.

19. Parliament: Gini coefficient here higher than countries which impose greater overall taxes, *The Straits Times*, 19 March 2018.

20. *Ministry of Finance*, Social spending increased from $20 billion in 2010 to $37 billion in 2019.

21. Kong Weng HO and Marcus Kheng Tat TAN, Challenges to social mobility in Singapore, July 2020. See also Income growth, inequality and mobility trends in Singapore, *Ministry of Finance*, August 2015 for the period between 2004 and 2014.

22. *The Straits Times*, Heng Swee Keat deeply concerned that Singaporean students lack drive, 1 February 2012.

23. *World Economic Forum*, ASEAN youth technology, skills and the future of work, August 2019. Only 17% of Singaporean youth would consider becoming an entrepreneur, compared to 35% in Indonesia, 31% in Thailand, 26% in Vietnam, and 23% in Malaysia.

24. *The Business Times*, Why more Singaporeans should consider a 'tour of duty' in overseas markets, 1 August 2022.

25. In 2017, out of S$850 billion of direct investments abroad, S$140 billion, or 16 percent, was made to China. *Source*: Department of Singapore Statistics 2018.

Chapter 3

1. Sweden complains it is collecting too much tax, *Financial Times*, 23 February 2017. Why Swedes overpay their taxes, *The Economist*, 23 February 2017.

2. *Ibid.*

3. Sweden ranked seventh in the 2023 edition of the World Happiness Index.

4. The only country that comes close to Sweden is China, but as we point out in *Values at the Core*, when asked the question of whether they generally trust others, many Chinese respondents believe that the question relates to people they already know.

5. European Social Survey, Round 10 (2022).

6. *Ibid.*

7. The shame of a Swedish Shopper (a Morality Tale), *New York Times*, 14 November 1995.

8. Raymond Fisman and Edward Miguel, Cultures of corruption: Evidence from diplomatic parking tickets, 2006.

9. Pomperipossa in Monismania, Astrid Lindgren, March 1976.

10. Medlingsinstitutet and the Swedish Ministry of Finance.

11. Jonas Agell *et al.*, Tax reform of the century — The Swedish experiment, December 1996.

12. Gunnar Du Rietz and Magnus Henrekson, Swedish wealth taxation, 1911–2007, 2015. Magnus Henrekson and Daniel Waldenström, Inheritance taxation in Sweden, 1885–2004: The role of ideology, family firms, and tax avoidance, February 2016.

13. Gunnar Du Rietz and Magnus Henrekson, (2015), *Op. cit.*

14. Gross domestic savings rate (% of GDP), *World Bank*, 2022.

15. Imports and exports of goods and services as % of GDP, *World Bank*, 2022.

16. Gross domestic spending on R&D, *OECD Data*, 2021.

17. Immigrant children in Sweden blamed for country's poor test scores, *The Independent*, 16 March 2016.

18. In 2022, according to the company's annual statements, Volvo sold 615,000 cars compared to less than 350,000 in 2009.

19. Annual report state-owned enterprises 2022, Government Offices of Sweden.

20. Orange report 2020, annual report of the Swedish pension system.

21. Employment — Annual statistics, Eurostat, 2022. The Netherlands has the highest employment rate in Europe with 82.9 percent, followed by Sweden with 82.2 percent. Age group 20–64.

22. Northern lights, *The Economist*, 2 February 2013. The employment rate in Sweden in 2022 was 82.2% according to Eurostat, behind the Netherlands at 82.9%.

23. Susanne Wallman Lundåsen, Lokalsamhälletillit i Sverige före och efter flyktingkrisen, March 2021. See also Local community interpersonal trust in Sweden before and after the refugee crisis on the European Commission website, March 2021.

24. *Reuters*, Sweden hits record with 60 shot dead in 2022, 19 December 2022.

Chapter 4

1. Botswana poverty assessment report, *The World Bank*, 2015.
2. Corruption perception index 2020, *Transparency International*.
3. Lekorwe *et al.*, Public attitudes toward democracy, governance and economic development in Botswana, *Afrobarometer*, 2001.
4. Jonathan Tepperman, The fix: How nations survive and thrive in a world in decline, 2016.
5. The education spending as a proportion of the GDP is calculated using figures from the 2022 Budget and GDP. The education spending as a proportion of total budget uses figures from the 2023 Budget presented to Parliament on 6 February 2023.
6. Secondary education statistics brief, *Statistics Botswana*, 2013.
7. *UNICEF Botswana*, Education budget brief, 2018.
8. Primary school performance in Botswana, Mozambique, Namibia, and South Africa, Nicholas Spaull, *SACMEQ*, September 2011.
9. Trends in Mathematics and science study, *The World Bank*, 2015.
10. Martin Carnoy, Linda Chisholm and Bagele Chilisa, The low achievement gap, 2012.
11. Paul Bennell *et al.*, The impact of the HIV/AIDS epidemic on the education sector in sub-Saharan Africa: A synthesis on the findings and recommendations of three country studies, 2002.
12. Jonathan Tepperman, The fix: How nations survive and thrive in a world in decline, 2016.
13. Botswana poverty assessment report, (2015), *Op. cit.*
14. Peter Guest, Diamonds aren't forever, *Forbes*, 1 December 2015.
15. Botswana diamond workers bleed, *Mail & Guardian*, 20 February 2015.
16. Botswana poverty assessment report, (2015), *Op. cit.*
17. Statistics Botswana, Formal sector employment survey, March 2016.
18. Lesego Sekwati, Economic diversification: The case of Botswana, 2010.
19. *Reuters*, Diamond sales at De Beers' Botswana unit rebound as global market recovers, 6 August 2021.
20. *El Pais*, Botswana's diamond trade, an increasingly lucrative business in one of the most unequal nations, 1 October 2023.

Chapter 5

1. Tirthankar Roy, Economic reforms and textile industry in India, August 1998.
2. S. V. Subramanian *et al.*, Sustainable development goal indicators in 707 districts of India: A quantitative mid-line assessment using the National Family Health Surveys, 2016 and 2021, June 2023.
3. Akash Kapur, India becoming: A portrait of life in modern India, 2012.
4. MOSPI gross state domestic product, ministry of statistics and programme implementation, 2017–2018.
5. *The Hindustan Times*, Delhi and Punjab richest states, Jain wealthiest community: National survey, 13 January 2018. *The Times of India*, Jains steal the show with 7 Padmas, 9 April 2015.
6. Economic survey report, 2021–2022.
7. T. N. Ninan, Turn of the tortoise: The challenge and promise of India's future, 2017.
8. India Services Sector, A multi-trillion dollar opportunity for global symbiotic growth, *Deloitte*, 2017.
9. Rachel M. McCleary, Salvation, damnation, and economic incentives, 2007.
10. Indian workforce prefers to be entrepreneurs: Survey, *Economic Times*, 9 August 2017.
11. The case for a 4-day workweek? Survey by the workforce institute at Kronos incorporated and future workplace, September 2018.
12. Race Disparity Audit, *Cabinet Office*, October 2017.
13. American Community Survey, S0201: Selected population profile in the United States, American Community Survey, *United States Census Bureau*, 2019.
14. *CNN*, The Indian migrants who built Kenya's "lunatic line," 11 December 2014. Live History India, *Laying The Lunatic Line*, 18 June 2018. Neither Kenya, Mozambique, Uganda, nor Tanzania publishes economic data by ethnic group. Their success is, however, documented in various press articles and scholarly publications, such as those of Gijsbert Oonk. The list of richest East Africans is compiled by *Forbes Magazine*.

15. A Himalayan challenge, *The Economist*, 11 October 2007. Jagdish Bhagwati and Arvind Panagariya, Why growth matters, 2013. *BBC News*, What ails the Indian economy? 26 September 2017.

16. Spectre of automation hangs over Indian manufacturing, *Financial Times*, 20 October 2015.

17. Devashish Mitra, Indian manufacturing: A slow sector in a rapidly growing economy, 2006.

18. T. N. Ninan, (2017), *Op. cit.*

19. India economic survey 2018: Farmers gain as agriculture mechanisation speeds up, but more R&D needed, *Financial Express*, 29 January 2018.

20. Republic of India: Accelerating agricultural productivity growth, *The World Bank*, 2014.

21. Most of India's state-owned firms are ripe for sale or closure, *The Economist*, 1 June 2017.

22. William W. Lewis, The power of productivity, 2004. *The Economic Times*, Discom debt surges 24% to Rs 6.2 lakh crore in 2021–2022, 11 April 2023.

23. UP foodgrain scam may require 5,000 FIRs, *The Times of India*, 9 December 2010 and India's immense 'food theft' scandal, *BBC News*, 22 February 2011.

24. In India the granaries are full but the poor are hungry, *The Guardian*, 7 September 2010.

25. Physician, heal thyself: How graft afflicted NRHM in UP, *The Hindu*, 18 October 2016.

26. *The Industan Times*, 'If you can't control corruption, legalize it', 18 August 2014.

27. Narayana Murthy, A better India: A better world, 2009.

28. Speech given on 25 September 2014.

29. World Values Survey, Most people can be trusted, 2014. India did not participate in subsequent rounds of surveys.

30. Poor PISA score: Govt blames 'disconnect' with India, *The Indian Express*, 3 September 2012.

31. Tanushree Chandra, Literacy in India: The gender and age dimension, 2019.

32. Annual Status of Education Report, 2018. *The Times of India*, 61% of Class 8 students can't do simple math, says survey, 16 January 2019.

33. UNICEF, India Statistics, quoted from Abhijit Banerjee, Esther Duflo, Poor economics: A radical rethinking of the way to fight global poverty, 2002.

34. Karthik Muralidharan, Jishnu Das, Alaka Holla, and Aakash Mohpal, The fiscal cost of weak governance: Evidence from teacher absence in India, 2016.

35. *Ibid.*

36. National Statistic Office, Second advance estimates of national income 2022–2023, Quarterly Estimates of Gross Domestic Product for the Third Quarter (Q3) of 2022–2023, 28 February 2023.

37. Reserve Bank of India, Foreign direct investment flows to India: Country-wise and industry-wise, 2017–2018. Mauritius accounts for 35 percent of all foreign direct investment, Singapore 25 percent.

38. *The Financial Express*, Remittances to India grew 26 percent to $112.5 billion in FY23, 14 August 2023. Remittances represented 2.8 percent of the GDP in 2022.

39. Ease of doing business 2020 rankings, *The World Bank*.

40. Digital India: Technology to transform a connected nation, *McKinsey Global Institute*, March 2019.

Chapter 6

1. GDP per person employed, constant 2011 PPP, International Labour Organization.

2. On February 2024, the Nikkei 225 index closed higher than the record set in 1989.

3. *Bloomberg*, Japan's fear of risk is getting dangerous, 6 December 2012.

4. *Ibid.*

5. Consumption share of purchasing power parity converted GDP per capita at current prices for Japan (*Source*: St Louis Fed).

6. Gross domestic savings (% of GDP), *The World Bank*.

7. *Nikkei Asia*, Japan has world's best passport, but few go abroad, 18 December 2019.

8. *The Japan Times*, 613,000 in Japan aged 40–64 are recluses, says first government survey of hikikomori, 29 March 2019. *CNN News*, Japan was already grappling with isolation and loneliness. The pandemic made it worse, 7 April 2023.

9. EF English Proficiency Index, 2017.

10. Ryoichi Mikitani and Hiroshi Mikitani, *The Power to Compete*, 2014.

11. Japan aims to double service-sector productivity growth, *Nikkei Asian Review*, 4 March 2016.

12. Niall Murtagh, The Blue-Eyed Salaryman, 2005.

13. *The Asahi Shimbun*, Death from overwork still leaving its stamp on corporate life, 20 July 2018.

14. PISA 2022 results.

15. World Values Survey Wave 7, 2017–2022.

16. Japan Automobile Manufacturers Association, The Motor Industry of Japan, 2023.

17. Levi Tilleman, The great race: The global quest for the car of the future, 2015.

18. *The New York Times*, Why Japan is holding back as the world rushes toward electric cars, 9 March 2021.

19. According to the Health and Welfare Ministry, in 2020, 840,000 babies were born and 1.38 million Japanese died. Pre-COVID-19, there were around 400,000 –450,000 more deaths than births.

20. Ministry of Finance 2008–2020.

Chapter 7

1. *CNN News*, Covid-19 drove hundreds of Africans out of Guangzhou. A generation of mixed-race children is their legacy, 18 March 2021.

2. Yang Yang, African traders in Guangzhou: Why they come, what they do, and how they live, 2011. Yang spent three months researching African traders in Guangdong, as part of her thesis for a master's degree in anthropology at the Chinese University of Hong Kong. See also Gordon

Mathews, African logistics agents and middlemen as cultural brokers in Guangzhou, 2015.

3. The World Bank in Nigeria, 3 November 2020.

4. *Annual Statistical Bulletin*, Organization of the petroleum exporting countries, 2022.

5. Paul Obi-Ani, Post-civil war political and economic reconstruction of Igbo land, 1970–1983, 2009.

6. Josephat Obi Oguejiofor, African Philosophy and the function of socio-political criticism: A skeptical consideration, 2004.

7. Chinua Achebe, *The Trouble with Nigeria*, 1998.

8. *The Guardian*, There was a country: A personal history of Biafra by Chinua Achebe — Review, 5 October 2012.

9. Gregory Emeka Chinweuba and Evaristus Chukwudi Ezeugwu, The ontological foundation of Igbo entrepreneurship: An analytical investigation, 2017. See also Lawrence Okwuosa, Chinyere T. Nwaoga, and Favour Uroko, The post-war era in Nigeria and the resilience of Igbo communal system, 2021.

10. Chinua Achebe, *Op. cit.*, 1998.

11. Imo and Abia states produce oil, but in very small quantities, accounting for 1 percent and 0.7 percent, respectively, of Nigeria's total oil production (*Source*: Nigerian National Bureau of Statistics).

12. *BudgIT*, State of States, 2022 edition, Subnational governance reforms for a new era. The states with a majority Igbo population are Anambra, Abia, Imo, Ebonyi, and Enugu. See also *The Economist Intelligence Unit*, GIDD, GDP per capita for each Nigerian state in real terms, 2018.

13. It is estimated that the Igbo language is spoken by about 225,000 people in the US, according to the US Census Bureau in 2019. According to the American Consumer Survey in 2019, there were 462,000 Nigerian Americans. According to the 2020 US Census, the median household income for Nigerian Americans was $71,467, compared to $74,932 for White Americans.

14. Osuo-Siseken, Uzoma Oguguo, and Uche Victor Uboh, State-based analysis of candidates' WASSCE participation and achievement of five credits passes and above including mathematics and English language in Nigeria, 2020.

15. *The Guardian Nigeria*, Despite decades of funding, literacy level in the northern states remains low, 24 July 2017.
16. Nigeria has become the poverty capital of the world, *Quartz Africa*, 25 June 2018.
17. *The World Bank*, Ease of doing business, 2020.
18. *Afrobarometer* Survey 2020, Round 8.
19. *Quartz Africa*, Why so many African Americans have Nigerian ancestry, 10 August 2020.
20. *The Economist*, Nigeria's economy is stuck in a rut, 15 May 2021.
21. 2021 American Community Survey. Median household income for those with Ghanaian ancestry was US$ 69,021 in 2020, compared to a median American household income of US$ 63,179.
22. *Afrobarometer*, Nigerians show high tolerance for diversity but low trust in fellow citizens, Afrobarometer study shows, 10 March 2021.

Chapter 8

1. How workers coped after GM shuttered its Janesville plant, *The Washington Post*, 20 April 2017.
2. Janesville-Beloit, WI metropolitan statistical area, *U.S. Bureau of Labor Statistics*.
3. Trump promised this Wisconsin town a manufacturing boom. It never arrived, *The Washington Post*, 22 August 2023.
4. Alexis de Tocqueville, Democracy in America, 1835.
5. David M. Tucker, The decline of thrift in America: Our cultural shift from saving to spending, 1991.
6. State offered $195 million in failed bid for GM plant, *Wisconsin State Journal*, 7 July 2009.
7. The growing gap in life expectancy by income: Implications for federal programs and policy responses, National Academies of Sciences, Engineering, and Medicine, 2015.
8. Lori G. Kletzer, Job losses from imports: Measuring the costs, 2001.

9. U.S. Private Sector Job Quality Index (JQI). The index went from 94 percent in 1990 to 85 percent in September 2023.

10. Arnaud Costinot and Andrés Rodríguez-Clare, The US gains from trade: Valuation using the demand for foreign factor services, 2018.

11. General Social Survey, proportion of respondents who answer positively to: Generally speaking, would you say that most people can be trusted or that you can't be too careful in dealing with people?

12. Robert D. Putnam, Bowling alone: The collapse and revival of American Community, 2000.

13. Public trust in government: 1958–2023, Pew Research Center.

14. Thomas Piketty, Emmanuel Saez and Stefanie Stantcheva, Optimal taxation of top labor incomes: A tale of three elasticities, 2014.

15. Business Insider, 4 million people quit their jobs in April, sparked by confidence they can find better work, 9 June 2021. Several studies claim that a UBI does not provide less of an incentive for people to work. Many of them are described in books such as Rutger Bregman, Utopia for Realists, 2017, and Abhijit Banerjee and Esther Duflo, Good economics for hard times, 2019. The experiments always follow the same pattern: A small group of people is given cash handouts over a few months, during which researchers assess how the cash is utilized and how the socioeconomic conditions of the beneficiaries have changed. Those experiments are done over a short period of time, often comprise few participants, and provide cash handouts that are usually not sufficient for beneficiaries to replace their income. But, most importantly, because the funds are only given to a small group of people, those people are incentivized to make good use of them over the duration of the experiment to make it a successful one in the hope that it will be expanded. Such small-scale experiments, in our view, provide a very misleading understanding of what would happen if a UBI was to be applied to an entire country or city for amounts close to what people currently earn.

16. Kara M. Reynolds and John S. Palatucci, Does trade adjustment assistance make a difference? 2008.

17. OECD Revenue Statistics 2020.

18. The federal revenue system: Facts and problems, *Joint Economic Committee*, 1956.
19. Federal Tax Receipts as a Percentage of GDP, Office of Management and Budget, 1945–2020. Federal tax receipts have remained within 15–20 percent of the GDP throughout America's modern history.
20. Employment by major industry sector, *Bureau of Labor Statistics*, 2022. Industry contribution to percentage change in real GDP, measured in real value added, *Bureau of Economic Analysis*, 2022.
21. Looking to the future, public sees an America in decline on many fronts, *Pew Research Center*, 21 March 2019.
22. Personal saving as a percentage of disposable personal income, U.S. Bureau of Economic Analysis. Savings rates for the nineteenth century were taken from David M. Tucker, The decline of thrift in America: Our cultural shift from saving to spending, 1991.
23. Steven Malanga, Whatever happened to the work ethic? *City Journal*, Summer 2009.
24. Gini Index, World Bank. China's index stood at 38.2 in 2019, whereas the index for the US was 39.7 in 2020 (latest years of available data).

Chapter 9

1. Sophie Meunier, A tale of two ports: The epic story of Chinese direct investment in the Greek Port of Piraeus, 14 December 2015.
2. China seeks dominance in Athens Harbor, *Spiegel Online*, 9 April 2015 and Under Chinese, a Greek Port thrives, *New York Times*, 10 October 2012.
3. China seeks dominance in Athens Harbor, (2015), *Op. cit.*
4. Yannis Palaiologos, The 13th labour of Hercules, *Inside the Greek Crisis*, 2015.
5. Tax Evasion in Greece, Ernst & Young, 2016 and Nikolaos Artavanis *et al.*, Tax evasion across industries, Soft credit evidence from Greece, September 2015.
6. AMECO 2000–2007, European Commission's directorate general for economic and financial affairs. See also Tax Shortfalls in Greece, Capó Servera and Georgios Moschovis, March 2008.

7. Tax Evasion in Greece, Ernst & Young and DiaNEOsis, 2016.

8. Tax Evasion in Greece, Ernst & Young, 2016, DiaNEOsis opinion poll.

9. Tax Evasion in Greece, (2016), *Op. cit.*

10. The cost of protecting Greece's public sector, *The New York Times*, 10 October 2012.

11. Greece's toothless battle against corruption, *Spiegel Online*, 17 November 2010.

12. *Eurostat*, Expenditure on pensions, 2015.

13. 2011 pension sustainability index, *Allianz*.

14. *Eurostat*, (2015), *Op. cit.*

15. *Ibid.*

16. Lois Labrianidis and Nikos Vogiatzis, Highly skilled migration: What differentiates the 'Brains' who are drained from those who return in the case of Greece? June 2012.

17. World Values Survey, Wave 7 (2017–2022). Only 8.5 percent of Greeks believed that most people can be trusted.

18. Katarzyna Growiec *et al.*, Social capital and the financial crisis: The case of Iceland, 2012.

19. *Eurobarometer*, April 2019.

20. *Eurostat*, Gini coefficient of equivalised disposable income — EU-SILC survey.

21. Doing Business 2009, Training for reform, Economic Profile Greece.

22. Greece: The cost of a bribe, *Transparency International*, 2012.

23. Doing Business 2020, Economic Profile Greece.

24. The expression is attributed to former Federal Reserve Chairman William McChesney Martin, in a speech made on 19 October 1955 for the Investment Bankers Association of America.

Chapter 10

1. The story is inspired by Guogang Lü, Behind the Chinese Miracle, 2012, a compilation of stories by migrant workers in China.

2. 2018 China Statistical Yearbook. The migrant population is referred to, in official statistics and by the overall population, as the "floating population."

3. An Xuehui, Teacher salaries and the shortage of high-quality teachers in China's rural primary and secondary schools, 2018. It should also be noted that only certain provinces in China take part in PISA rankings and that all are located along the eastern coast. A truly national PISA ranking would likely show lower results given the fact that coastal provinces are generally more economically developed than those in the western or northern parts of the country.

4. Richard Burkholder and Raksha Arora, Is China's famed "work ethic" waning? 2005.

5. Young Chinese are sick of working long hours, *BBC News*, 10 May 2018.

6. Zuo Qiuming, *Zuo Zhuan*, fifth century BC.

7. Gross fixed capital formation, *World Bank*, 2021.

8. Arthur R. Kroeber, China's economy, what everyone needs to know, 2016.

9. Shaun Rein, The war for China's wallet, 2017.

10. China's debt mountain scales new heights on trade war stimulus, *Nikkei Asian Review*, 19 June 2019.

11. S&P Global Ratings, Global debt leverage: Is a great reset coming? 2022 figures.

12. George Magnus, Red flags: Why Xi's China is in Jeopardy, 2018.

13. Moody's quarterly China shadow banking monitor, March 2019.

14. China's shadow banking sector shrinks sharply amid continued regulatory oversight, *The Asian Banker*, 31 March 2022.

15. Does China face a looming debt crisis? *China Power*, 7 September 2017.

16. China's latest financial threat: Surging consumer credit, *Caixin Global*, 6 November 2018.

17. Georges Haour and Max von Zedtwitz, Created in China: How China is becoming a global innovator, 2016.

18. *World Bank*, Starting a Business Index, May 2020. In 2021, the World Bank decided to discontinue this annual report. *Reuters*, Georgieva pressured World Bank employees to favor China in report — ethics probe, 17 September 2021.

19. Keyu Jin, The new China playbook: Beyond socialism and capitalism, 2023.

Chapter 11

1. Taylor Branch, The Clinton Tapes: Wrestling history with the President, 2009.
2. *Reuters*, Russia's Yeltsin known for gaffes, off-color jokes, 2007.
3. Aleksandr Korzhakov, Boris Yeltsin: From Dawn to Dusk, 1997. See also a review of the book by Thomas de Waal, *London Review of Books*, 1998.
4. *Forbes Magazine*, Russian edition, 19 April 2012.
5. Tamara Men, Paul Brennan, Paolo Boffetta, and David Zaridze, Russian mortality trends for 1991–2001: Analysis by cause and region, 2003.
6. Alexei Kudrin and Evsey Gurvich, A new growth model for the Russian economy, 2015.
7. *Ibid.*
8. Gregor Feifer, *Russians*, 2014.
9. *Ibid.*
10. Gabriel Di Bella, Oksana Dynnikova, and Slavi T. Slavov, The Russian state's size and its footprint: Have they increased? 2019.
11. Alexei Kudrin and Evsey Gurvich, A new growth model for the Russian economy, 2015.
12. Jake Cordell, Why is Russia so unproductive? 23 September 2019.
13. *McKinsey Quarterly*, How Russia could be more productive, 2009.
14. World Values Survey, Wave 7, 2017–2022.
15. *Transparency International*, Corruption perceptions index 2020.
16. Gregory Kisunko and Steve Knack, The many faces of corruption in the Russian Federation, 22 April 2013.
17. *Gini Index*, World Bank estimate, 2020. Credit Suisse, Global Wealth Report 2020.
18. PISA 2018 results. Russia did not participate in 2022.
19. Full list can be found on www.NoblePrize.org.
20. Loren Graham, Lonely ideas: Can Russia compete? 2013.
21. Skolkovo projects show effective state-business partnership in high-tech sector, *TASS*, 16 December 2020. The Skolkovo Foundation: Fostering

innovation and entrepreneurship in the Russian Federation, *WIPO Magazine*, September 2020.

22. *The Moscow Times*, Business environment in Russia worse than 1990s, say half of executives, 2019.

23. Leons G. Taivans, Russia on the threshold: Orthodox tradition and protestant ethics, 2001.

24. World Values Survey, *Op. cit.*, percentage of respondents who provide answers of 1–4 to the question: 'On a scale of 1–10, with 1 meaning you agree completely with the statement and 10 meaning you disagree completely, does hard work bring success?'

25. Russia's fatalism has fatal consequences against COVID-19, *The Daily Beast*, 20 April 2020.

Chapter 12

1. *New York Times*, Sultan of Muscat and Oman is overthrown by Son, 27 July 1970.

2. Matthew Gray, The economy of the Gulf States (World Economies), 2019.

3. *The Economist*, Sultan Qaboos, ruler of Oman for almost 50 years, has died, 11 January 2020. The number of motor vehicles registered comes from Donald Hawley, *Oman and its Renaissance*, 1977.

4. Mark Curtis, The great deception: Anglo-American power and world order, 1998.

5. *History Today*, The Sultan, the Imam and the question of Oman, 2 July 2020.

6. *The Economist*, *Op. cit.*

7. Nasser Al-Mawali, Haslifah Mohamad Hasim, and Khalil Al-Busaidi, Modeling the impact of the oil sector on the economy of Sultanate of Oman, 2016.

8. World Happiness Report, 2015. Oman, together with several other Gulf countries, was not included in rankings after 2015.

9. According to Oman's National Center for Statistics & Information, the country's GINI coefficient for 2018 was 30.75. The corresponding figures for France and Germany in 2021 were 31.6 and 31.9, respectively. No data beyond 2018 are available for Oman.

10. BP Statistical Review of World Energy 2020.

11. Oman Investment Authority, Kuwait Investment Authority, Public Investment Fund, Investment Corporation of Dubai, Abu Dhabi Investment Authority, Mubadala Investment Company, 2022 reports.

12. The Arab Gulf States Institute in Washington, Natural gas in Oman: Too much of a good thing? 26 December 2019.

13. *Oman Daily Observer*, Oman's total fish production surges 38pc to nearly 800,000 MT in 2020, 4 March 2021. Manaa Alhabsi and Nik Hashim Nik Mustapha, Fisheries sustainability in Oman, 2011.

14. *Times of Oman*, Oman education: Gender parity in education a positive sign, 18 March 2017. Women make up 58 percent of all university graduates.

15. Matthew Gray, (2019), *Op. cit.*

16. Daniel Yergin, The new map: Energy, climate, and the clash of nations, 2021.

17. This raises the question as to why the citizens of Arab countries devoid of natural resources do not have a more positive attitude toward work. We will not speculate on those reasons given the absence of any noteworthy research done on this topic.

18. *Arabian Business*, 56% of Arabs do not work: Gallup study, 19 August 2013.

19. Julanda S. H. Al-Hashmi, Rifts in Omani employment culture: Merging joblessness in the context of uneven development, 2019.

Conclusion

1. Caroline Hickman, Elizabeth Marks, Panu Pihkala, Susan Clayton, Eric R. Lewandowski, Elouise E. Mayall, Britt Wray, Catriona Mellor, and Lise van

Susteren, Young people's voices on climate anxiety, government betrayal and moral injury: A global phenomenon, 2021.

2. Andrew McAfee, *More from Less*, 2019.

3. *Pew Research Center*, Social trust in advanced economies is lower among young people and those with less education, 3 December 2020.

4. *CBS7*, FBI calling stabbing at Midland Sam's a hate crime, 31 March 2020.

5. *France24*, How foreigners, especially blacks, became unwanted in parts of China in the midst of the COVID crisis, 29 April 2020.

6. Daniel Voyer and Susan D. Voyer, Gender differences in scholastic achievement: A meta-analysis, 2014.

7. *The Atlantic*, Why girls tend to get better grades than boys do, 18 September 2014.

8. Angela Lee Duckworth and Martin E. P. Seligman, Self-discipline gives girls the edge: Gender in self-discipline, grades, and achievement test scores, 2006.

9. UNESCO Institute for Statistics, School enrollment, tertiary, female (% gross), 1970–2022.

10. *Gallup*, Two-thirds of young Arab women remain out of workforce, 2 April 2012.

Printed in the United States
by Baker & Taylor Publisher Services